Eight Chinese Plays

from the thirteenth century to the present

Also by William Dolby

A History of Chinese Drama

Translated with an Introduction by William Dolby
'The Perfect Lady by Mistake' and other stories
by Feng Menglong (1574–1646)

Eight Chinese Plays

from the thirteenth century
to the present

Translated with an Introduction by
WILLIAM DOLBY

Columbia University Press New York
Paul Elek London
1978

Copyright © 1978 William Dolby

All rights reserved

Published in 1978 in Great Britain by Elek Books Limited

and in the United States of America by Columbia University Press

Printed in Great Britain

Library of Congress Cataloging in Publication Data

Main entry under title:

Eight Chinese plays from the thirteenth century to the
   present.

   Includes bibliographical references.
   CONTENTS: The battling doctors: excerpt from Cai
Shun shares the mulberries (Cai Shun fen-shen): yuanben
play attributed to Lin Tangqing. – Grandee's son takes
the wrong career (Huan-men zi-do cuo li-shen). [etc.]
   1. Chinese drama – Translations into English.
   2. English drama – Translations from Chinese.   I. Dolby,
   A.W.E.
PL2658.E5E37   1978   895.1'2'008   77-15601

ISBN 0-231-04488-7

Contents

Introduction

In 1894 a Westerner with twenty-two years experience of China remarked:

> We must take account of the fact that [...] the Chinese have a strong dramatic instinct. The theatre may almost be said to be the national amusement, and the Chinese have for theatricals a passion like that of the Englishman for athletics, or the Spaniard for bull-fights. [...] A Chinese thinks in theatrical terms. [...] If his troubles are adjusted he speaks of himself as having 'got off the stage' with credit, and if they are not adjusted he finds no way to 'retire from the stage'.[1]

These observations may embody some sweeping generalizations, but they are echoed in many other Western writings on China. Nor indeed is there a lack of Chinese evidence for the pervading influence of the theatre upon Chinese life.

The beginnings of Chinese theatre are to a large extent lost in the mists of time.[2] From what evidence has survived they seem to have come remarkably late for a civilization with such a long, continuous and ancient culture. During the Tang dynasty (618–907) and the Five Dynasties (907–60) there flourished slapstick plays called *canjunxi*, 'Adjutant plays', and during the Sòng (960–1279) and Jin (1115–1234, ruling the northern part of China conquered from the Sòng) dynasties – partly as a development from the *canjunxi* – arose the kinds of play known as Sòng *zaju*, 'variety plays' (including the *guanben zaju*, 'official-text variety plays') and Jin *yuanben*, 'entertainer texts' or 'singing-girls' quarters' texts'.

The Sòng *zaju* and the *yuanben* were, as far as we can tell, similar in themes and form, being fairly brief and structurally simple farces or slapstick comedies. Although they are readily recognizable as theatre, they are not perhaps what we would usually label 'drama' in the more special sense of the word. Most of what we know about them comes from literature of the thirteenth century and later, and from plays of the Yuan (1234–1368) and Ming (1368–1644) dynasties. No examples of such plays survive from the Sòng or Jin dynasties, but a few – either described as *yuanben* or closely following the probable form of

7

yuanben – are included in longer plays of the Yuan and Ming periods and also elsewhere in Ming literature. The example translated in this collection[3] under the title *The battling doctors* is a comic interlude inserted in the drama *Cai Shun shares the mulberries*, a play attributed to Liu Tangqing of the Yuan period which survives as a late Ming manuscript. The comic clash between medical men was a feature inserted in other dramas of the Yuan and Ming periods, and seems to have existed as an independent *yuanben* during the Jin. Our example shows many of the characteristics that we believe to have been common to many of the Sòng *zaju* and Jin *yuanben*: the essentially slapstick framework of a verbal and physical combat between knave and butt, or between two clowns, with medical bags serving for the usual padded cudgel (*kegua*, the equivalent of the Western fool's bauble, slapstick, lath sword, or bladder filled with peas), the climactic quickfire exchange in verse, the coarse roguery, and so forth. In Europe, one may reflect, the connection between clowning and mountebankery was often very close, as for instance in seventeenth-century France in the case of the actor Tabarin, whose fooling helped his brother the quack doctor Mondor to sell his nostrums, and of Jean Farine, the quack doctor who turned stage buffoon. Molière trenchantly laid bare the fallibilities and foibles of medical practice, and likewise in China the medical doctor was a ready target for comedy, usually appearing either as a farcically incompetent rascal or as a grimly amusing villain. It is to be noted that some of the early playwrights of China were doctors in real life or were otherwise associated with the medical profession.

In *The battling doctors* the rather unusual device of the interlocutor is used. It is found in other early plays, but was not necessarily a general feature of *yuanben*. It is in fact used extensively elsewhere in *Cai Shun shares the mulberries*, from which this extract is taken. Seemingly the function of the interlocutor is to punctuate and emphasize the humour, and to intensify the contrast between the doctors' roguery and shocked common sense and decency, expressed in the form of exclamations and questions that might well echo the audience's reactions.

During the Sòng dynasty, possibly as a side-shoot or parallel development of the Sòng *zaju* mentioned above, there came into being during the years 1119–25 a kind of play variously known as Wenzhou *zaju* or Yongjia *zaju*, Wenzhou and Yongjia being the names of its place of origin. After the non-Chinese Jin dynasty (founded by the Jurched people) conquered the northern parts of China in 1117, this kind of play flourished in the region of the Yangtse basin, the 'southern' heartland of ancient China, and maintained its popularity there until the 1270s. In the early thirteenth century it may still not have been a mature, complex form of drama, but around the middle of that century there developed in the northern parts of China, beyond the Sòng domains, the kind of drama known as Yuan *zaju*, which is generally regarded as the earliest form of true drama in China. When, in the 1270s, the rulers of the north conquered the Sòng and reunited the whole of China under one rule, it was the northern drama which dominated the nation's theatre as a whole. The southern style continued to be performed, however. During the middle of the fourteenth century it underwent a revival, in a form heavily influenced by the Yuan *zaju*. By the late thirteenth or early fourteenth century it had become a complex drama-form, which is nowadays generally referred to as *nanxi* ('southern plays') or *xiwen* ('play texts') drama. During the Ming period the southern form of drama, the *chuanqi* ('marvel play'), a more literary, and formally more regulated kind of *nanxi*, came in turn to dominate the northern *zaju* as the prevalent national drama, and for centuries the northern *zaju* and southern *chuanqi* came to be regarded as the two main styles and forms of Chinese written plays.

Our present example of *nanxi*, *Grandee's son takes the wrong career*,[4] by an anonymous 'genius' (i.e. playwright) of Hangzhou, is interesting as much for its contribution to the history of Chinese drama as for its story. Very few *nanxi* survive as anything like complete plays, and this is the second or third earliest such survival, most probably from the mid-Yuan period. It gives a vivid insight into the theatrical world of those days, the attitudes of society towards the theatre, the life of the actors and the relationship between *yuanben*, Yuan *zaju* and *nanxi*. It concerns performers of Yuan *zaju* and *yuanben* and is set in the north of China during the Jin dynasty, two of the leading characters having Jurched names. The Jin dynasty setting is a strong reminder that those who, like myself, have tended to regard the Yuan *zaju* as originating during the Yuan dynasty can only regard this theory as a tentative one; but there may have been other reasons for the Jin setting. Most evidence points firmly towards the origin of the form during the Yuan period. The Jin setting may have been a deliberate attempt to avoid mentioning the Yuan, but this would surely have struck contemporaries as an odd distortion. It does not seem likely from the contents of the play that the characters were Jurcheds under the Yuan. A Yuan *zaju* of the same title was composed by Li Zhifu, a Jurched whose Jurched name was Pucha Li Wu. Among the eleven plays attributed to him was a Yuan *zaju* called *Tiger-head shield*, in which some of the leading characters were Jurcheds. Another playwright, Zhao Wenyin, wrote a Yuan *zaju* of the same title which was a 'second version' of Li's play. Zhao, who went by the professional name of 'Bright Mirror' (he was probably an actor as well) was a Comptroller of Entertainers of the imperial Music Academy and was thus in charge of actors and singing-girl entertainers. Both he and Li Zhifu belonged to the first phase of Yuan *zaju* playwrights and almost certainly produced their plays either before 1300 or not much after that date.

The *nanxi* play *Grandee's son takes the wrong career*, given its Jurched setting, was almost certainly an adaptation of one or both of these Yuan *zaju*. From the various Yuan *zaju* mentioned within the play, which are mostly early or mid-Yuan, it would seem a fair guess to say that this *nanxi* was written between the 1320s and 1340s. It is typical of both *nanxi* and *chuanqi* drama in a number of ways: the prologue, the large number of acts (these are not actually marked in the text, but my act divisions seem fairly reliable from the structure), the prosody of verses (rhyming according to southern pronunciations and being closer to the old *ci* genre of poetic composition which had originated in the Tang dynasty and prevailed longer in the south as a popular form), the sharing of the singing between a number of characters, and so forth. The love-theme, too, fits in well with the southern tradition, since a much greater proportion of *nanxi* and *chuanqi* are based on love-themes than is the case with Yuan *zaju*. Verse occupies a large part of the translated text, and in actual performance the dialogue and action, especially towards the end of the play, must have been much fuller than we are able to show. The sparseness of the text, along with some printing or copyist errors and other obscurities, allow of only a provisional translation at certain points, but we have here, nonetheless, one of the earliest substantial Chinese plays to survive.

Why China's first mature drama should have arisen in the north of China is a much debated question. The *yuanben* and other kinds of popular entertainment, such as the *guzici*, 'drum lyric',and *zhugongdiao*, 'key medley' or 'mode medley', ballads (ballads containing song interspersed with prose speech), puppetry and oral story-telling, had already led to the development of a large body of performers, of stage facilities, attractive techniques of presentation, and an audience familiar with a vast range of tunes and tales. But the vital step of transition from slapstick plays, comic duos, simple saucy sketches, and song-and-dance acts to a complex drama, wide-ranging in its thematic capacity, seems to have been connected with the Mongol conquest of the Jin of northern China in 1234.

To suggest such a precise date would seem to smack of over-simplification, but it must be remembered how decisive that date was in so many ways, for China and for the world. As mentioned above, it has been suggested that 'Yuan' *zaju* began during the Jin. Indeed, many of the leading earliest playwrights of 'Yuan' *zaju* were Jurcheds or had strong connections with or loyalties to the defunct dynasty after the Mongol conquest. Mongol and other far northern cultural influences were felt, no doubt sometimes very strongly, in Jin China even before 1234, but from the evidence we have it is difficult to avoid the conclusion that the conquest itself was the vital factor. Most writings on the topic assert that when the Chinese scholar-class was largely denied its traditional access to government posts under the hostile Mongol regime, or when, as was often the case, its members simply refused to serve the conquerors, many scholars sought another outlet for their educational abilities and their frustrations in the world of drama. There would seem to be at least some truth in this theory, but the possibility that positive contributions were also made by the Mongols and their allies should perhaps be given far more attention than hitherto. The evidence is sparse, but there are indications that the Mongols, and many of the allies who joined them in the conquest, were well disposed towards singing and popular entertainments such as play-acting and story-telling, partly as a means of contacting Chinese civilization. By this favourable attitude the Mongols may have both encouraged stimuli from outside China and also have removed certain barriers to the development of popular entertainments within China, barriers including the traditional Chinese orthodox prejudice against the involvement of scholars in such activities, which also limited government approval of them. The more austere aspects of Confucianism tended to restrain the lusty eclecticism and indeed the broad and coarse humour of the theatre, though this restraint might often have been no more than an overt disapproval concealing a secret delight. The overturn of the considerably sinicized Jin regime must have created a new, more fluid situation in this respect which may well have been for the benefit of the drama. We can maintain with fair confidence that it was in the Mongol capital of Dadu – present-day Peking – or its environs that China's first great drama world came into being.

Our translation of a Yuan *zaju*, *Qiu Hu tries to seduce his own wife*,[5] is by Shi Junbao, the author of ten plays, and one of the earliest known playwrights. He seems to be identifiable with a certain

Shizhan Junbao (1192–1276), *alias* Shizhan Deyu. This Shizhan Deyu was a handsome man, noted as a dutiful and loving son and for his high moral standards, and a close friend of that great man of letters Wang Yun (1227–76). A painter of fame, he also for some while pursued a military career, in which he rose to responsible rank as a commanding officer. He was a Jurched, his surname Shizhan being a Jurched one. Such polysyllabic Jurched names were often rendered into one-syllable Chinese surnames. His national origins and the early period at which he lived provide further evidence of how debatable is the period of origin of Yuan *zaju* drama. The play survives in a seventeenth-century edition, which almost certainly embodies a great deal of Ming editing, but the core of the play – that is, its songs and the pattern of its plot – may be largely Shi Junbao's original composition.

The story of Qiu Hu is found in many early pieces of Chinese literature. Its earliest known sources are the *Memoirs on virtuous women* attributed to Liu Xiang (77 BC–6 BC) and the *Miscellaneous notes on the Western Capital* attributed variously to his younger brother Liu Xin (c.53 BC–23 BC), Ge Hong (c.250–c.330) and Wu Jun (469–520). Both of these works give short anecdotes stressing the chaste steadfastness of Qiu Hu's wife and ending with her suicide. Many poets also used or mentioned the tale. During the Tang dynasty there was a narrative chantefable (*bianwen*) on the theme. Our play also uses a similar story about the Maid Luofu (hence the heroine's family name Luo) who boldly refused a nobleman's advances. This tale is first found in the *Ancient and modern notes* by Cui Bao (fl.c.AD 300).

The imperial family of the Ming Dynasty who drove the Mongol regime from China were from the beginning considerable patrons of drama. Two imperial princes became notable playwrights of Yuan-style *zaju*, and in the early decades of the Ming the Yuan-style *zaju* flourished, at least in the circles surrounding the throne. But the new imperial house came from the south, and by their conquest of the whole country they contributed to trends in favour of southern cultural influences, trends that had already been well under way in the late Yuan, when not only had the centre of *zaju* production moved south to the Hangzhou region but the southern *nanxi* had also undergone a great revival. During the late fifteenth and early sixteenth centuries the southern drama, by now considerably influenced by the northern *zaju*, had acquired further esteem through being written by playwrights who were eminent orthodox literary and political figures. Now, as what we generally refer to as *chuanqi* drama, it seems to have become the most vigorous national form.

In the middle of the sixteenth century a new epoch for *chuanqi* drama was initiated by various noted singers and musical masters who combined to create a new form of music which was used in its performance. This music blended much in the northern and southern traditions, absorbing northern and southern tunes, 'northern vigour' and 'southern mellifluousness', its flexibility, eclectic comprehensiveness and stress on sound rather than word-matching constituting its chief novelty. Intended to be popular and universal, this music was appropriated by the socially lofty and 'highbrow'. It was known as Kunshan-*qiang*, and the *chuanqi* drama performed to this music became known as Kunqu ('Kun songs'). Soon the Kunqu style of singing and associated styles of acting and performance came to be considered the most elevated kind of theatre. To this day, Kunqu singing is considered the most classical or 'highbrow' music of the Chinese theatre.

Chuanqi were often very long plays, sometimes of more than forty acts. At some periods they were performed whole, on successive days, but the most common practice has been to perform extracts from them as independent plays, sometimes two or three acts being performed, but more often than not just one act.

Our translated example from the *chuanqi* is *Secret liaison with Chancellor Bo Pi*,[6] which is Act VII from the play *Washing silk* by Liang Chenyu (1520–80 or later), written about 1579, a famous drama which was the first to establish the popularity of Kunshan-*qiang* as a musical style for theatre performance. The play as a whole tells of the ancient conflicts between the kings of the states of Wu and Yue during the Spring and Autumn period (770–481 BC). It is based on material originating from the first millennium BC, in particular the account in the *Historical records* of Sima Qian (147–*c*.90 BC), and on a wealth of earlier literature. The stories associated with this conflict have been a rich source of inspiration to Chinese literature throughout the ages, and even before Liang's play there were poems, stories, *bianwen*, Yuan *zaju* and other plays utilizing them. In the act translated here, advance forces from Wu under the comic villainous Chancellor Bo Pi are attacking the Yue capital, Kuaiji, which is in a perilous condition. The noble minister of Yue, Wen Zhong, is undertaking an embassy to the Chancellor in an attempt to bribe him with gifts and buy off the doom of Yue and the King of Yue.

In the sixteenth and early seventeenth centuries a great surge of literary and publishing interest resulted in the appearance of several collections of edited and expanded Yuan *zaju* (also including some early Ming *zaju*, these sometimes being perhaps in a more pristine state). This helped to perpetuate the influence of the *zaju* form on creative activities, and in the late Ming many playwrights wrote both *zaju* and *chuanqi*. The term *zaju*, however, must be used more loosely in connection with the works of this period. Often it meant a play with the same general four-act or five-act shape and with the same structure as the Yuan *zaju*, though with the infusion of distinct southern features, but in addition the term *zaju* came to refer to short plays of one or two acts, different in both length and scope from the Yuan *zaju*. Some early examples of the latter type were in fact described as *yuanben*, but they had perhaps even less connection with what we know of Jin and Yuan *yuanben* than with Yuan *zaju*. This brief *zaju* was a convenient mode for the expression of simply plotted but often witty or sophisticated themes, and several lively plays of this kind were written from the mid-Ming (fifteenth century) onwards. The '*yuanben*' *Wolf of Mount Zhong*[7] by Wang Jiusi (1468–1551), written around 1510, was one of the earliest of these 'brief *zaju*'. Wang obtained his doctorate in 1496 and served in the government, rising to the high rank of Ministerial Secretary in the Ministry of Civil Office. He and his friend the playwright Kang Hai (1475–1540) were both accused of being associates of the disgraced eunuch official Liu Qin (*d.*1510) and suffered as a consequence. Kang Hai also wrote a *Wolf of Mount Zhong* play, his version being a full four-act *zaju*, regarded as a satire against a person whom he viewed as responsible for some of his troubles. Wang's play, too, may well have been a satire. The other play he wrote, *Roaming in the spring*, was said to be a satire against the prime minister, Li Dongyang (1447–1516). Jiusi was known as one of the Ten Geniuses of his age. His *Wolf of Mount Zhong* uses a tale that is found in various forms in many other parts of the world. Xie Liang (Sòng dynasty) wrote a *Story of the Wolf of Mount Zhong* and perhaps his tale was the inspiration for the plays. Ma Zhongxi (*d.c.*1512), who obtained his doctorate in 1475 and was at one point jailed for his opposition to Liu Qin, also wrote a tale with the same title. This was also considered a satire by some, but – as with so many pieces of ancient Chinese literature – specific satire was seen in something that may well have been no more or less than a generalized exposure of a universal human failing, or simply an entertaining story.

Under the Qing dynasty (1644–1911) there was an increasingly diversified pattern of drama development, the fate of the theatre being governed to a considerable extent by lavish imperial patronage coupled with stern imperial surveillance. The early decades of the dynasty seem rather like a twilight of the Ming theatre, although a full and eventful one, and some of the finest *chuanqi* were created during this period. Afterwards, the actor seems greatly to overshadow the playwright. There was an increasing tendency to perform short *zaju* or one-act selections, often farcical or risqué sketches. The moral atmosphere of the metropolitan theatre became more openly lax, partly no doubt in reaction to social and legal strictures against actresses, and this tendency culminated in the vogue for the female impersonators Wei Changsheng and Chen Yinguan in the 1770s and 1780s, a vogue not restricted to the capital. Other kinds of theatre also flourished in the provinces, where from the late Ming onwards the range and variety of local and regional styles of performance steadily increased, *chuanqi* and *zaju* being written and adapted for several other styles besides Kunqu. Imperial birthday celebrations and other reasons also brought regional styles to the capital. *Buying rouge*,[8] a one-act *zaju* written to be performed with the styles of music and acting known as Bangzi-*qiang* and Chui-*qiang*, was popular there in the late eighteenth and early nineteenth centuries. It is fairly typical in length and manner of many others of the time, which included vigorous battle scenes, knockabout buffoonery and saucy suggestive pieces. For all their lightness of plot they were eminently stageable, requiring a small cast and being packed with action. They were also very convenient as light accompaniment to graver and loftier dramas. In comparison with the latter, plays like this contain relatively little song. The element of action predominates. *Buying rouge* seems ultimately to derive from a prose story found in a collection compiled in AD 977. There is a Yuan *zaju* called *Leaving the slipper* by an unknown playwright, and also a Yuan or early Ming *nanxi*, both based on the same general story, which is that of the love affair of Guo Hua and Moon Beauty: how he commits suicide for love of her, how she is charged with the responsibility for his death but, weeping brokenly beside him, manages to revive him, and how they are happily united in marriage.

The major theatrical event of the nineteenth century was the emergence of the genre of drama internationally known as Peking Opera. This had its roots in much earlier forms of theatre and entertainment, but its 'birth' may reasonably be placed around 1830, when the first major steps were taken in the process of synthesizing various regional styles of music and performance into this composite genre. The process was well under way by the middle of the century, the latter decades of which saw a golden age of Peking Opera. The genre continued to prosper in the twentieth century as the main traditional form of Chinese drama. Its popularity was nationwide and its celebrity extended throughout the world. Our translation of a Peking Opera, *Hegemon King's farewell to his queen*,[9] is from one of the best-loved and most important works in this form, and since its historical setting is so vital to an appreciation of this often terse play, we shall consider this in some detail.

The play concerns Xiang Yu (232–02 BC), the historical Hegemon King of Chu, his vital struggle with Liu Bang, King of Han and later founder of the Han dynasty (206 BC–AD 220), and his resounding fall from power. The topic has been a fertile one for Chinese literature of all kinds. When China's first powerfully centralized empire, that of the totalitarian Qin dynasty (221–07 BC), broke up, various rebel warlords attempted to re-establish the independent kingdoms into which China had formerly been divided. Xiang Yu became the most powerful of these rebels, hence his title Hegemon King. In one of the most tantalizing 'ifs' of history, he might have succeeded in making himself the ruler of all China, and indeed he largely created the political and military situation that enabled the Han dynasty to establish itself so firmly and enduringly. But although a man of enormous physical strength and outstanding valour and prowess, he erred in his impetuosity, his lack of planning, and his frequent inability to heed good advice. Yet he is generally depicted as altogether a more noble and heroic figure than his rival, the coarse, anti-intellectual, often devious Liu Bang.

A man from the region of the present-day province of Kiangsu, Xiang Yu was from a family that for generations had produced generals for the Kingdom of Chu, situated in the Yangtse basin in the mid-south of China. His father had led forth eight thousand young men from Kiangsu to attack the Qin. Xiang Yu, after becoming the most powerful of the new kings and princes, committed various grave errors of judgement. For instance, his nostalgia for the south led him to set up his capital there, whereas a more northerly location would have been psychologically and strategically more sound. And on more than one occasion when he seemingly had Liu Bang at his mercy, he allowed him to escape. Eventually, short of food for his forces, Xiang felt obliged to conclude a treaty with Liu, whereby they divided China (their 'world', in effect) into two spheres of domination, the dividing frontier between them running along Goose Ditch, a tributary of the River Bian in Honan province. Xiang Yu was to hold sway over the territory to the east, and Liu Bang over that to the west of Goose Ditch. At the same time, he restored to Liu the latter's wife and children whom he had captured.

The following year, Liu Bang and various other princes who had joined him fought and routed Xiang Yu at Gaixia, 'Borderfoot'. Xiang Yu heard Chu songs being sung in the Han camp, and assumed that Han had already conquered the land of Chu. He rose during the night and began drinking wine, his company including his beautiful consort, Queen Yu, and his faithful, magnificent steed, Dapple. Then he sang his famous song, 'I've the strength to uproot mountains', etc. (as in the play). After he had sung it several times Queen Yu joined in and they sang it as a duet. All present wept. Shortly afterwards, he broke through the enemy encirclement with a small force but, mindful of the sorry fate of the army of eight thousand young men of Kiangsu who had supported his cause, he felt ashamed to face the elders of Kiangsu again and, refusing to seize an opportunity of escaping across the Raven River (in Anhwei province) to Kiangsu, abandoned all further flight. Among his pursuers he recognized Lü Matong, a Han cavalry marshal and former comrade of his. 'Aren't you an old friend of mine?' he said to Lü. '[...] I have heard that Han is offering a reward of ten thousand gold pieces and a feoff of ten thousand households for my head. I shall do you a good turn.' Whereupon he cut his own throat and died.

Xiang Yu's early biographer, Sima Qian, from whom much of the above information derives, in summarizing his impressions of him, says:

Yu seized the chance and rose in the wilds, and within three years he led the Five Monarchs of the states of Qi, Zhao, Han, Wei and Yan to the destruction of Qin, divided up the world into feoffs for the various princes, with himself as the arbiter of major policy, and gave himself the title of Hegemon King. Although his throne did not endure, in the whole of history there has never been his like. When [Xiang] Yu abandoned Guan[-zhong][10] in his longings for Chu, banished the Honorary Emperor[11] and set himself up as [supreme] ruler, thus causing the princes to turn against him in indignation, he placed himself in a virtually impossible situation. Possessing an overweening boastful pride in his own great deeds, deeming his personal wisdom to be perfectly adequate, and taking no lessons from the past, he regarded the Hegemonship as something to be accomplished by force [alone]. He it was who determined the course of the world, yet within five years his dynasty had fallen and he himself had met his death at Dongcheng,[12] but to the end he had not awoken to realities. Still he would not blame himself for anything. That was where his error lay. When he made the excuse, 'Heaven is ruining me. It is not that I went wrong in the conduct of my campaigns', he was talking nonsense and no mistake![13]

Our Peking Opera makes considerable use of ancient historical accounts, and indeed often uses their language verbatim or only slightly altered. It also derives much from earlier literature and legends, in particular from the long novel *Saga of the Western Han*, attributed to Zhong Xiang (*d.* 1625). Many earlier plays were written about Xiang Yu, including two Yuan *zaju* by thirteenth-century playwrights: Gao Wenxiu's *Hegemon King lifts the cauldrons* and Zhang Shiqi's *Hegemon King says farewell to Queen Yu at Borderfoot*.

This Peking Opera, a favourite piece of the famous actor Mei Lanfang's, stresses Xiang Yu's erratic moods and impetuosity, his generous credulity, his wild courage, his blindness to good counsel and weakness for bad, and his love for Queen Yu and his charger Raven Dapple. Queen Yu is in many ways the leading character of the play. She is the very model of tender concern and loving fidelity, and when her wise advice fails she tries to the end to comfort, cheer and aid Xiang Yu, thinking only of his well-being. The play is basically a love-poem, in which the momentousness of the historical tragedy (in the dramatic sense) intensifies the personal drama.

The large area and cultural diversity of China have encouraged the emergence of a wide range of local styles and variations of theatrical performance. All the more national forms of Chinese traditional drama were at one time or other regional forms, and throughout the history of Chinese drama there have been competition, interplay and interinfluence between national and localized forms of theatre. New kinds of drama have continued to be created into present times. The distinctions between the various genres of theatre have been rather in the manner of presentation, music, costume, make-up, dialect and acting techniques than in the subject-matter, although there are many kinds of drama with their own special and markedly distinct themes. There has been widespread use of the same plays and a sharing of time-venerated topics, and even when new plays have appeared on new themes they have often spread very rapidly from one kind of drama to another. The theme of the regional play *Identifying footprints in the snow*,[14] and much of its wording, are used by other genres of drama, too, and have a long history, but I translate from a Chinese version performed in a regional style as recently as the 1950s. It is a Chuanju play, Chuanju being a generic name for various types of dramatic performance current from as early as the Ming dynasty in Szechwan province in the far west of China, one of the most vigorous regions for Chinese theatre since the Ming dynasty. There were a Jin or Yuan *yuanben*, three Yuan *zaju* (Guan Hanqing's *Tumbledown kiln*, Wang Shifu's play of the same title, the latter being still extant, and Ma Zhiyuan's *After-meal bell*) and one or more fourteenth- or fifteenth-century *nanxi* on the general story that is the background of this play. It is a tale of how the poor young scholar Lü Mengzheng and a wealthy young beauty, turned from her father's door, go to live together in a tumbledown kiln, from which the young man often has to venture out in fierce snowstorms to beg for food at a temple, etc. A Lü Mengzheng (946–1011) actually lived during the early Sòng dynasty and came out Top Graduate in the imperial examinations of 977, and some of the events of his life would seem to have suggested the original story used by the plays. The original written source was most probably the biography of Lü Mengzheng in the official *History of the Sòng* written by Ouyang Xuan (1273–1357) and others and produced in 1345. Jiang Yikui (late sixteenth to early seventeenth century) in his *Extra records of Yaoshan Study* also reproduced the tale. Ye Sheng (1420–74) in his *Diary of east of the water* notes the popularity of the story as a drama in his times. The present play is based to a considerable extent on Act XII of an anonymous early Ming *nanxi* called *Many-coloured bower* and often borrows its wording, but has superimposed its own mood and sparkle.

William Dolby

'The battling doctors'

Excerpt from *Cai Shun shares the mulberries*:
Yuanben play attributed to Liu Tangqing
(late thirteenth or early fourteenth century)

Characters:
DOCTOR FINISHEMOFF : physician.
INTERLOCUTOR.
DOCTOR MUDDLY HEAD : physician.
SQUIRE CAI : wealthy literatus.
LADY CAI : Squire Cai's elderly mother.

(Enter Doctor Finishemoff.)

DOCTOR FINISHEMOFF.
> I am a Grand Physician, a doctor of high degree,
> versed in pulse and prescription, a very ocean of education ;
> when people call me in to attend to their malady,
> I tell them to cart the coffin out by way of preparation.

I'm Doctor Finishemoff, and my medical treatments have a unique quality all of their own.

> My forbears have all been physicians,
> I've been polished and trimmed in the best of traditions.
> I'm a dab-hand at playing guitar
> and bellowing fine operā ;
> Fine wines 'tis my hobby to quaff,
> plump geese 'tis my pleasure to scoff.
> When invalids call me, my tonic
> leaves them feeling decidedly chronic ;
> On my physic few thrive –
> far more fail to survive.

INTERLOCUTOR. *(Chips in)* And that's no idle boasting! Cor blimey!

DOCTOR FINISHEMOFF. I've a colleague in the trade, a physician by the name of Muddly Head. Turnip Head is his old man's name. My therapeutic techniques fit in well with theirs, so Muddly Head and I have sworn eternal brotherhood and joined up in partnership with one another. If either of us is called out to examine a case, we always go together – we refuse to go alone. I diagnose the illness and he gives the medicine, or else he does the diagnosis and I give the treatment. We've both taken an oath: if either of us secretly attends the sick on his own, may he be stricken with ulcers of the mouth!

Well, today a local squire, Scholar Cai, has been here to seek my services. He said that his mother was ill, and would I prescribe some medicine. I've sent a man round for my good friend, and I'm now waiting for him here on Zhou Bridge. He should be coming any moment now.

(*Enter Doctor Muddly Head.*)

DOCTOR MUDDLY HEAD.
I'm a comforting friendly physician,
and supremely reputed in my medical capacity;
The cordials I concoct, the potions I prescribe,
are simply supernatural in unfailing efficacity.
That Bian Que, famous Leech of Lu in grey antiquity,
was just a raw beginner in comparison with me!
Why, when sufferers call me in to remedy their plight
with a single teeny tablet I can douse them like a light.

INTERLOCUTOR. (*Chips in*) That's enough, you rogue!

DOCTOR MUDDLY HEAD. Your humble servant is a medical doctor, name of Head, Muddly Head. When I was little, they used to call me Pin Head. We've had medical practitioners in my family for three generations now, and in the matter of healing arts
I'm unclear as to medical lore,
the pharmacopoeia's beyond my ken.
When I'm called to a patient I pour
three noggins to start with and then
a couple of pots of vintage wine,
add five mutton-and-onion fritters,
swallow the lot and in no time
it'll send you decidedly crackers.
No good for the patient, of course I know that,
but it keeps me well-stocked with fodder and liquors!

INTERLOCUTOR. (*Chips in*) My word, what a marvellous pair you two make!

DOCTOR MUDDLY HEAD. I've a colleague in the medical profession, a certain physician by the name of Finishemoff. His remedial techniques concur excellently with mine, and for that reason we've sworn eternal brotherhood with one another, he in the role of elder brother and myself as the younger brother. If either of us is called out to a case, both of us insist on going together. If one of us is missing, it's no go. Head won't go without Finishemoff, and Finishemoff won't go without Head, so from start to finish Head has never started off without Finishemoff, nor has Finishemoff headed off ahead of Head.

INTERLOCUTOR. (*Chips in*) Ooh, what awful puns! Cut it out!

DOCTOR MUDDLY HEAD. This morning Finishemoff sent his man round for me, with word that Scholar Cai's mother was ill and would I go and see to her. Well, my good friend's waiting at Zhou Bridge, so I must be off there to join him. Ah, here I am. (*Greets Finishemoff*) Ah, elder brother! Please accept my apologies for turning up so late. Don't take offence, and if you do, you're a toad's bastard!

INTERLOCUTOR. (*Chips in*) Cut it out, you rogue!

DOCTOR FINISHEMOFF. You've got a cheek, talking like that! You're always making out it's not your fault. This cold winter weather, making me wait here so long! I'm so freezing I've got leg-cramps.

DOCTOR MUDDLY HEAD. Come now, good friend. Don't hold it against me for coming so late: I've been suffering from a spot of heartburn and I got up a bit earlier than usual this morning and was affected by the chilly air. Oh, the pain of it, it nearly killed me! My wife was at her wits' end. She called a doctor round, and he gave me a dose of medicine, which stopped the pain.

INTERLOCUTOR. (*Chips in*) You're a doctor yourself: why on earth do you have to get your medicine from another doctor?

DOCTOR MUDDLY HEAD. If my medicine was any good, I'd have taken it.

INTERLOCUTOR. (*Chips in*) What do you mean, it's no good?

DOCTOR MUDDLY HEAD. If I'd taken my own medicine, I'd be two hours dead by now.

INTERLOCUTOR. (*Chips in*) You a Hippocrates and won't take your own medicine! Cut it out!

DOCTOR FINISHEMOFF. Younger brother, ever since we fought that legal case, we've done no trade whatsoever.

INTERLOCUTOR. (*Chips in*) Why did you fight a law case?

DOCTOR FINISHEMOFF. We cured someone to death.

INTERLOCUTOR. (*Chips in*) What a pair of glib bletherers! Cut it out!

DOCTOR FINISHEMOFF. Doctor Head, my good friend, today His Worship Cai's old mum is ill, and he's asked us to go and apply our remedies. They're a very wealthy family, so when we get there, if she's hardly ill at all, we must say she's rather ill, and if she's rather ill, we must say she's extremely ill. Ah yes, when we get there, we'll wade into her with the acupuncture and moxibustion, give her a dose of physic, and

> If she's restored
> we'll demand a great hoard
> of cash and of paper in pay;
> Should she suddenly slump,
> our Gladstones we'll hump
> and take to our heels straight away.

INTERLOCUTOR. (*Chips in*) Cut it out, you rogue!

DOCTOR MUDDLY HEAD. Doctor Finishemoff, my good friend, your suggestions are most apposite. Heaven will not let two such thoroughly good chaps as us go short of their modicum of nosh.

INTERLOCUTOR. (*Chips in*) You can say that again!

DOCTOR FINISHEMOFF. Well, my friend, let's go. Ah, here we are now. You! Announce us. Tell your master that two wonder-physicians have arrived.

BUTLER. Just wait here, and I'll go and announce you. (*Announces them*) Beg to inform you, your honour, that the doctors have come.

SQUIRE CAI. Tell them to please come in.

BUTLER. Yessir. Please come in.

DOCTOR MUDDLY HEAD. Colleague, take a hold of yourself. Don't collapse.

INTERLOCUTOR. (*Chips in*) Eh, what's up?

DOCTOR MUDDLY HEAD. They've asked us in! They've asked us in!

INTERLOCUTOR. (*Chips in*) What's all the fuss? Come off it!

DOCTOR FINISHEMOFF. We're government registered gentlemen physicians, and if we put ourselves out to come and attend to them in their home, they must come out ànd welcome us in the proper manner, not just tell us to come on in!

INTERLOCUTOR. (*Chips in*) Don't hold it against him: he's got a sick mother. Go on in, eh?

DOCTOR FINISHEMOFF. Good lad! For your sake, then, I shall go in.

INTERLOCUTOR. (*Chips in*) The fellow does play high and mighty! Cut it out!

DOCTOR FINISHEMOFF. (*Standing back*) You first, dear colleague.

DOCTOR MUDDLY HEAD. How could I? No, after you, my elder brother.

DOCTOR FINISHEMOFF. No, after you, my noble younger brother.

DOCTOR MUDDLY HEAD. You are in error, my elder brother, my senior! You know, although I, your humble servant, do not study the Confucian and Mencian scriptures, I am fully acquainted with the ethical proprieties practised by the ancient Kings of Virtue. Surely you must have heard that our Holy Sage, Confucius, says: 'He who walks slowly behind his seniors is said to have due younger-brotherly reverence, while he who rushes on ahead of his seniors is said to be irreverent. When tillers give way on the paths or travellers make way on the roads, the senior is accorded the role of elder brother while the younger is accorded that of younger brother.' Now you, elder brother, are my senior, and I'm your younger brother. Given this difference of seniority, there must be a due apportioning of respect. Verily the ancient Kings of Virtue were perfectly correct in their rules of etiquette! And should I go in before you, I would be an ass, a swine, a thorough hypocrite!

INTERLOCUTOR. (*Chips in*) What a load of high-flown chatter! Cut it out!

DOCTOR MUDDLY HEAD. No, I can't. I simply can't. You first, dear colleague.

DOCTOR FINISHEMOFF. No, I couldn't think of it. You, my noble younger brother, are a true gentleman of virtue and bounty, while I am but a clumsy dolt. I, insignificant creature that I am, am not worth one inch of straw, while you, superior soul, possess virtue as copious as the Nine Rivers. When you, my younger brother, apply your therapy to people's illnesses, your treatments are divinely successful, and you command an abundance of excellent nostrums for the containment of malady. Yes, you, my dear young colleague, are a paragon of erudition, whereas I am a mere maggot's skin. Were I to go in ahead of you, then I, mere pupil that I am, would truly be like unto a dog's bone!

INTERLOCUTOR. (*Chips in*) Cut it out! Load of twaddle! Go on in, now!

(*They go in and see Lady Cai.*)

DOCTOR FINISHEMOFF.
Dear Madam, you are ailing, suffering a debilitation,
DOCTOR MUDDLY HEAD.
Your doctors with their physic will dispel your tribulation.

(*Finishemoff grasps her left hand and Muddly Head grasps her right hand.*)

DOCTOR FINISHEMOFF.
See now how your doctors in concert test your pulse's
palpitation.

(*Raising her left hand, sings*)

We test the nuances of her pulse the moment we step through
the door,
DOCTOR MUDDLY HEAD. (*Raising her right hand, sings*)
She's so thin and wasted her wrist resembles a stalk of
hempen straw.
DOCTOR FINISHEMOFF. (*Sings*)
Let us hurry and open our medical packs,
DOCTOR MUDDLY HEAD. Alas, poor lady, her pulse feels bad.
(*Sings*) and for the shops make speedy tracks.
DOCTOR FINISHEMOFF. (*Sings*)
Yes, for the shops make speedy tracks.
SQUIRE CAI. What for, doctors?
DOCTOR FINISHEMOFF. (*Sings*)

25

To buy her a coffin, to buy her a box.
DOCTOR MUDDLY HEAD. (*Sings*)
To buy her a coffin, to buy her a box.
INTERLOCUTOR. (*Chips in*) Won't you ever give up? Cut it out!

(*Doctor Finishemoff knocks Lady Cai flat with his Gladstone bag.*)

LADY CAI. Help, he's beating me to death!
INTERLOCUTOR. (*Chips in*) What on earth are you doing, hitting an invalid like her?
DOCTOR FINISHEMOFF. Don't worry. Don't worry. She can't be so bad: she's still sensitive to pain!
INTERLOCUTOR. (*Chips in*) 'Otherwise she'd die', eh? Cut it out!
DOCTOR FINISHEMOFF. Mister Head, sir! What is the nature of her illness?
DOCTOR MUDDLY HEAD. My dear colleague, far be it from me to vaunt my powers of diagnosis, but I have just this moment completed my perusal of her appearance and my examination of her pulse, and you will remark, if you feel her body on this side, that it is burning like fire – She's suffering from a fever.
DOCTOR FINISHEMOFF. There you go, talking rubbish again. Her pulse is leaping an inch high. How can you say it's a fever? Just look at her over on this side: her body's as cold as ice. She's suffering from a chill.
DOCTOR MUDDLY HEAD. This poses no problem, dear colleague. If we take the old lady's nose as our starting point of frontier demarcation, we can tie a string round her nose, and pull the string down and tie it to a peg which we shall fix in the floor, to serve as a border between us. Then you treat her left side for chill, while I treat this right side of her for fever. How does that solution suit you, my friend?
DOCTOR FINISHEMOFF. Excellent! Excellent! That clarifies the position between us. But supposing that when the old lady takes the medicine you prescribe her it kills the right side of her, what then?
DOCTOR MUDDLY HEAD. That will in no way bother you in your treatment of the left side for chill.
DOCTOR FINISHEMOFF. Quite right, quite right!
DOCTOR MUDDLY HEAD. But then what if your dose of medicine for the old lady kills the left side of her?
DOCTOR FINISHEMOFF. That will in no way bother you in your treatment of her right side for fever.
DOCTOR MUDDLY HEAD. No, I mean, supposing both of us slip up, and our treatments kill both sides?
DOCTOR FINISHEMOFF. Then neither of us will be bothered.

INTERLOCUTOR. (*Chips in*) You blabbering whoresons! Cut it out!

SQUIRE CAI. Physicians! Come, what medicines are you going to give her now?

DOCTOR FINISHEMOFF. I am now about to give her a reviver tablet, then a lethal pill.

SQUIRE CAI. Why those two medicines?

DOCTOR FINISHEMOFF. Ah, let me explain: it is my intention by giving the old lady *both* these medicines to keep her from either dying ... or recovering!

INTERLOCUTOR. (*Chips in*) Cut it out, you rogue!

DOCTOR MUDDLY HEAD. Squire Cai, your honour, do you want this venerable lady of yours to get better?

SQUIRE CAI. Of course I want her to get better!

DOCTOR MUDDLY HEAD. I have a wonder-cure, but would you be willing to part with one of the ingredients it requires?

SQUIRE CAI. To help my mother recover, I'll gladly part with anything whatsoever that you may ask for.

DOCTOR MUDDLY HEAD. Well, scoop your eyes out with a sharp pen-knife. Drunk with a goblet of hot wine, they'll make your mother right as rain.

SQUIRE CAI. She may get well, but what about me?

DOCTOR MUDDLY HEAD. Ah yes, now, I think you'll need a white stick.

INTERLOCUTOR. (*Chips in*) Cut it out! Load of rubbish you talk, you villain!

SQUIRE CAI. Stop! Stop! Stop! Both of you cease your silly hullabaloo! Let whichever of you two gentlemen is in fact the most able doctor apply his remedies now.

(*Both doctors pick up their Gladstone bags and proceed to swap blows with the bags as they recite.*)

DOCTOR FINISHEMOFF. (*Hitting Head*)
    I'm clever at correcting contagions of all seasons,
DOCTOR MUDDLY HEAD. (*Hitting Finishemoff*)
    I medicate with mastery all manner of morbidity;
DOCTOR FINISHEMOFF.
    I cure infant vomiting, diarrhoea, anaemia and convulsions,
DOCTOR MUDDLY HEAD.
    I look after ladies in labour and post-natality.
DOCTOR FINISHEMOFF.
    I can doctor the four limbs and pulses all eight,
DOCTOR MUDDLY HEAD.
    I can treat the Five Wasting Diseases and Seven Debilitations;
DOCTOR FINISHEMOFF.

I remedy palsy of the left and paralysis of the right,
DOCTOR MUDDLY HEAD.
I rectify rapid consumptions and also slow consumptions.
DOCTOR FINISHEMOFF.
I can relieve, in either thigh, soreness or numb misery,
DOCTOR MUDDLY HEAD.
I can remove, from any limb, all dullness or torpidity;
DOCTOR FINISHEMOFF.
I can heal the mouth of acidity, the tongue of tart asperity,
DOCTOR MUDDLY HEAD.
I can chase from chest or diaphragm any blockage or
    languidity.
DOCTOR FINISHEMOFF.
I can mend lame legs and crippled arms,
DOCTOR MUDDLY HEAD.
I can make dumb men speak and deaf men hear again;
DOCTOR FINISHEMOFF.
I can banish chills and fevers with my balms,
DOCTOR MUDDLY HEAD.
I can make the backward forward and the crazy to think clear
    again.
DOCTOR FINISHEMOFF.
I can quell quinsy and dispel dropsy,
DOCTOR MUDDLY HEAD.
I can free the headache sufferers and the sinusitis-prone;
DOCTOR FINISHEMOFF.
I can cure bunions on the breast,
DOCTOR MUDDLY HEAD.
I can cure corns on the collar-bone.
DOCTOR FINISHEMOFF.
Your honour, by means of our medicine,
DOCTOR MUDDLY HEAD.
we'll free the old lady from mortal coil;
DOCTOR FINISHEMOFF.
Take a cup of cold water, full to the brim,
DOCTOR MUDDLY HEAD.
add half a pint of croton-oil.
DOCTOR FINISHEMOFF.
Tell the old lady to swallow it down,
DOCTOR MUDDLY HEAD.
it'll rack her belly with collywobbles;
DOCTOR FINISHEMOFF.
Straightway her innards'll stiffen and strain,
DOCTOR MUDDLY HEAD. (*Knocking Lady Cai flat with his Gladstone bag*)

yes, we'll purge your mum to death and eliminate further
troubles!
INTERLOCUTOR. (*Chips in*) You villainous sons of bitches! Clear off,
now! Clear off! (*Beats two doctors off stage.*)

Grandee's son takes the wrong career

'newly written by a genius of Hangchow'

Nanxi play: anon., late thirteenth or early fourteenth century

Characters:

PROLOGUE.

WANYAN SHOUMA: young Jurched scholar and nobleman, of Bianliang in Honan prefecture.

VALET: Wanyan Shouma's manservant.

DOGSON: steward or butler of the Wanyan household.

ASSISTANT PREFECT WANYAN: Jurched, father of Shouma, governor of Honan prefecture.

ZHAO RUBY PLUM: former actress, mother of Wang Golden Notice.

WANG GOLDEN NOTICE: beautiful young actress, from Dongping.

WANG SISHEN: father of Golden Notice, husband of Ruby Plum, and manager of their troupe.

IMPERIAL MESSENGER.

TEA-HOUSE KEEPER.

JING-CLOWN: in some unnamed role.

KNAVE (*Mo*-male-role): in some unnamed role.

CHOU-CLOWN: in some unnamed role.

PAGE: of Assistant Prefect Wanyan.

Preliminary titles:

> A roving actress tours the towns and cities,
> A handsome beau roams the land all o'er;
> A common stage-player plies her art,
> A grandee's son takes the wrong career.

[*Act One*]

PROLOGUE. Wanyan Shouma dwells in the Western Capital,[1] a dashing ardent blade and rapier wit, and there he meets the vaudeville actress Wang Golden Notice, which leads to his father's driving her away. He becomes a strolling player, all for the love of a beautiful woman, and uses all his gold and jewels until he has not a farthing left. Noble sirs, I bid you hush to watch us perform this *Grandee's son takes the wrong career*.

[*Act Two*]

WANYAN SHOUMA. (*Sings*)

Age after age we have worn clasp and tassel of noble degree,
of a lofty mandarin family I'm the posterity.
But how could I bear, like the sons of moneyed parvenus,
to study the ancient scriptures of verse and history!
I have no inclination for polished preciosity:
When halcyon days are here, all round the year
we must relish them in their entirety.

(*Says*)

I've always been bold and free,
petty convention has never shackled me;
I match the Plume Grove[2] in creativity:
from my hand, as a million pecks of jewels, my writing flows,
one bouquet of blossoms gay and gallant are my poetry and
    prose.
Genius gathers in my breast its brocade splendours,
sublime is my air as the shimmering moon and fresh zephyrs,
exalted my looks as verdant aleurites and emerald
    paulownias.
In plucking the lilies – in loving the ladies,
I yield nought in gallantry to Liu Shiqing;[3]
My breeze-and-moonlight romantic compositions
surpass, I would claim, the Gaffer of Duling.[4]

I'm Wanyan Shouma. My father is from the Jurched people and at
present holds the post of Assistant Prefect of Honan prefecture. A
little while ago a vaudeville actress from Dongping called Wang
Golden Notice came and gave a performance here. When I set
eyes on her, she somehow seemed like a seraph of highest heaven,
an angel of fairest paradise. She has the kind of face to 'still the
darting fishes and drop the winging swans in flight' and her looks
'eclipse the moon and shame all the flowers'. Had she but magpies
fluttering above her head, she would appear to be some goddess
descending from the Jasper Pool of heaven, and if a rabbit were to
run by her side she would seem no less fair than the Moon Fairy
leaving her Lunar Palace.[5] Of late, she and I have been having a
little affair. I just can't stop seeing her, so I'm going to go behind
my father's back and send a servant to invite her here into my
study quarters, so that we may relive the ecstasies of love together.
Oh, what a wonderful thing that will be! Valet!

VALET.

One shout from the master's end of the hall
brings a hundred 'yessirs' from the lackeys' gallery.

(Performs. [Actions of entering and greeting Shouma?] Wanyan Shouma tells him to go on the errand. Valet performs. [Gestures of refusal, prevarication or fear?])

WANYAN SHOUMA. *(Sings)*
>Stop now, just listen:
>go and bring my dainty charmer Golden Notice here to me.
>I'll be waiting for her in this study,
>– no 'mansions of the noble impenetrable as the depths of the
>   sea'!
>Tell her mother to entertain no suspicion,
>simply tell her there's a reception
>and a sumptuous feast for the guests is all laid;
>she must send her daughter in urgent speed.

VALET. *[This verse is probably recited rather than sung]*
>Young master, I beg you hear my advice:
>she's only a mere female mummer,
>so what's the point of such fuss and bother?
>All day moping and fretting your head,
>desperate to get her into your bed!
>I'm afraid your father will rebuke you fiercely,
>and then you'll repent your reckless folly
>in bringing disgrace on your noble family.

WANYAN SHOUMA. Well, if you won't go, call Dogson the steward in here to see me.

(Valet calls steward.)

DOGSON. *(Sings)*
>When the lord and master's not at home,
>I feel decidedly tickled;
>hey, audience, don't you know who I am?
>– I'm a little old professional cuckold.[6]

(Says)
>I've served here since I was a little boy,
>I'm all the family's pride and joy.
>Many a job I've fixed for your father,
>the ins and outs I know them all;
>and now I'm old I'm at your service,
>to attend to your needs whenever you call.
>If it comes to playing pander
>I'm peerless in my tricks;
>and anyway, if I refuse
>they baste me till I'm dropping bricks!

VALET. Steward, the young master's calling for you.

(*Dogson performs.* [*Gestures indicating alarm, or agreement?*] *Performs actions of going. Performs actions of meeting Shouma.*)

WANYAN SHOUMA. Go off to the theatre for me now, and tell Golden Notice to come here to my study quarters so that I can have a word with her.
DOGSON. I can go all right, but I'm just worried in case your father gets wind of it and I land in trouble.

(*Wanyan Shouma performs.* [*Pleading, or threatening gestures?*])

DOGSON. I know what to say.

(*Wanyan Shouma performs.*[*Gestures of gratitude or hastening Dogson on his way?*])

DOGSON. (*Says*)
  I'm the old family steward,
  I have to play sly for my daily bread;
  I'll expect you to manage meat and wine
  if you want me to wangle your bird to bed.
  If His Worship should get to know about it,
  it'll mean a thorough dose of wallops;
  he'll scoop the young girl's —
  and dock young master's bollocks.

(*Valet rounds off.*[*Significance unclear. Possibly a slapstick act, or quick-fire comic verse patter.*])

WANYAN SHOUMA.
  Now just make haste and go, don't tarry,
  I'll be waiting for her in my study.
DOGSON.
  If the lady won't come after all,
  just have a little fiddle on your beddy.
  (*Exeunt together.*)

[*Act Three*]

(*Enter Assistant Prefect Wanyan.*)

ASSISTANT PREFECT WANYAN. (*Sings*)
  How grateful I am to my emperor for conferring this weighty
    post on me;
  Throughout the Western Capital I enjoy celebrity,

yet I govern with whole-hearted impartiality,
in utmost fairness, with no disparity,
my integrity pure as water,
true in my judgements as the mirror's clarity,
bright as shimmering ice in my perspicacity.

(*Says*)
Now, I was born of the Jurched nation,
and in the Wèstern Capital conduct administration;
my father was the premier formerly,
I'm the scion of a line of mandarin nobility.
I surpass Sima[7] in promoting ordered domestic morality,
I excel Pang Juan[8] of yore in effecting the monarch's decree;
and as immaculate I direct my staff and wield my power
as the autumn-night moon that walks the clear mirror.

I'm Wanyan, the present incumbent of the assistant-prefectureship in Honan Prefectural Capital – the nation's Western Capital, that is. I've an only son, Wanyan Shouma, whom I've told to spend every day in his study, but these last few days I've not been to visit him in the study quarters. This morning I instructed Dogson to keep an eye on my son and make sure that he got up to no wild pranks, warning him not to facilitate any imprudent designs my son might entertain. But now I really ought to go and give the boy some encouragement in person to spur him on, before I go to preside over my court. Now,
Traveller, as you go, don't sing too loud,
lest you alarm the rustics beyond the wood.

[*Act Four*]

ZHAO RUBY PLUM. (*Sings*)
Once I was an actress, till, too suddenly, I saw
my locks and tresses at my temples tinged with hoar;
and now my only daughter plies the selfsame trade,
as if her choice of livelihood was Providence-made.

(*Says*)
From childhood I was an actress
and dwelt among the player men;
matched in keys are my melodies, my verses well wed to
   tunes,
and my lyrics, life-true, commune with the mysteries of Zen.

I'm Zhao Ruby Plum. Now that I'm getting on in years I depend for my keep on my only daughter, who earns us our living by performing plays. We come from Dongping, but we've brought our daughter here to the capital of Honan prefecture, and she's now been acting here for a good few days. We hung out the poster[9] this morning, so now I must call her and discuss the *zaju* ['variety play'] for tomorrow. Daughter! Come here!

GOLDEN NOTICE. (*Sings*)
> I'm just a young girl in the green spring of youth,
> but the star of the towns, widely celebrated;
> I've brought new life to the theatre, topsy-turvied its
>   conventions.
> and whenever I act on stage I'm adulated.

(*Says*)Ten thousand blessings upon you, mother.

RUBY PLUM. The reason I wanted you here, my child, was to discuss the matter of our daily bread with you, to decide what *zaju* to perform tomorrow.

GOLDEN NOTICE. I'm not feeling well today. I feel too listless to go to the theatre.

RUBY PLUM. But your dad has already gone to arrange things on stage.

GOLDEN NOTICE. No, I'm not feeling well. I can't go.

RUBY PLUM. (*Sings*)
> I beg you, child, just listen to me:
> get your things ready and speedily!
> The poster's been hung up already,
> and here you're behaving so awkwardly.
> What you think you're up to, I can't see!
> What you think you're up to, I can't see!
> You put your mother in such a fury:
> we depend for our keep on you,
> and letting the audience down won't do!

GOLDEN NOTICE. (*Sings*)
> I beg you, mother, listen to me:
> I tell you plainly
> I'm not refusing just to be awkward,
> I really am feeling rather poorly.
> If you keep on badgering, trying to force me,
> what on earth will I feel like then?
> Let them wait till the red wheel drops from the sky,
> – who cares if we let the audience down!

(*Enter Wang Sishen.*)

35

SISHEN.

> I've been to the theatre and got things ready,
> now what's up at home with the family?
> Look here, daughter, was that your worry:
> did you think you'd been summoned for government duty?[10]
> Now both of you cease your idle bickering;
> you, wife, stop your prating;
> the theatre-goers [lit. 'war-horses'] are packing the houses,
> we can't keep the audience waiting!

DOGSON.

> I've just been given an assignation,
> and here I am at my destination.

Here I am at their house now.

> His Worship is throwing a party,
> so cancel your theatre today;
> yes, cancel your theatre today,
> no need to get anything ready.
> – Quickly, quickly be on your way.
> No dilly-dally or delay,
> none of your silly stuff,
> or else I'll cut up rough.

RUBY PLUM *and* SISHEN. Are you sure it's His Worship who's sent for us?

DOGSON. You don't imagine I'd ever tell a fib?

GOLDEN NOTICE. I can't go. But I can't not go.

SISHEN. You go on ahead with the old steward, daughter, and I'll gather the props together and come straight on after.

DOGSON. No need for any props. It's only for singing excerpts from plays.

RUBY PLUM *and* SISHEN.

> Well then, daughter, you go on ahead,
> we'll go to the theatre instead
> to send the audience packing
> before we come and watch you singing.
> Now, daughter, be on your best behaviour:
> it's a banquet in His Worship's chamber.

GOLDEN NOTICE

> That's how things are, what use is it to bother?

TOGETHER.

> All we can do is 'drift on the wind' together.

(*Exeunt.*)

[*Act Five*]

WANYAN SHOUMA.(*Sings*)
It's an age since I sent word to my dear,
still the messenger's not reported back here.
DOGSON.
Back I race to report, in flurry and fear.
GOLDEN NOTICE.
Oh to see my love, and fulfill my desire!

(*They meet.*)

WANYAN SHOUMA. You've been just like Xiao He who wouldn't go to the feast – impossible to get.[11]
GOLDEN NOTICE. And when I, blind fool that I am, sought you, Little Sheep Brother, you were impossible to meet.[12]
DOGSON. 'Grows sadness of fall along the spine' – you were impossible to get in.[13]
WANYAN SHOUMA. I haven't seen you these last few days, young lady.
GOLDEN NOTICE. I wanted to come here, but was afraid in case His Worship your father got to know.
WANYAN SHOUMA. Well, without my father's knowing, I told this man to invite you here to my study quarters, so that we could have a tête-à-tête.
GOLDEN NOTICE. (*Sings*)
I look so worn and drawn because you've been swotting
those what-do-you-call-them classics in your study all these
days;
WANYAN SHOUMA. (*Sings*)
Let's not talk about such things, they just don't matter,
just hand me over the latest popular plays.
GOLDEN NOTICE. (*Sings*)
Here are the play-books, look,
and run through them with me to revise.
(*Says*) It's all you want to do all the time: sing songs! If His Worship your father hears of it, it'll be no joke.
WANYAN SHOUMA. Don't worry. Let's go once through the play-books you've brought.
GOLDEN NOTICE. You! Come here! I've something I want you to do for us.

(*Dogson goes and watches at the door.*)

37

GOLDEN NOTICE. (*Sings*)
> Listen now while I tell you all about them one by one:
>   there's a *Faithless Wang Kui*,[14]
> Meng Jiang Maiden goes a thousand miles *Delivering winter*
>   *clothing*,[15]
> Cloud Lady from the portrait as a *Ghost plays matchmaker*,[16]
> The *Love-birds' meeting*[17] of Miss Zhuo,
> *Guo Hua* makes an excuse of *Buying rouge*,[18]
> The girl Jewel Lotus is raised on board from the waves,
> and has a reunion at a *Riverside travel-halt*.[19]
>
> This play is *Grand Captain Zhou Bo*,[20]
> This play is *Cui Hu seeks water*,[21]
> This play is *Qiu Hu tries to seduce his own wife*,[22]
> This play is *Great Prince Guan goes alone to the single-sword*
>   *meeting*,[23]
> This play is *Horses trampling Lady Yang*.[24]
>
> *Liu Shiqing at Mancheng travel-halt*,[25]
> *The story of Zhang Gong and the west wing*,[26]
> *Killing a dog to reform a husband*,[27]
> *Maid Jing four times does not know*,[28]
> *Zhang Xie hacks at Poor Maiden*,[29]
> *Princess Lechang*,[30]
> Throwing 'green-plum' blossoms *Over the wall and on*
>   *horseback*,[31]
> Composing novel poetry in *Brocade Perfume Pavilion*,[32]
> His tryst arranged all by a handkerchief,
> *Monk Hong delivers a letter wrongly*,[33]
> *Lü Mengzheng amid a snowstorm in a broken-down kiln*,[34]
> *Yang Shi meets Han Jewel Child*,[35]
> Bitter injustice is requited in *Sole Heir of the Zhao clan*.[36]
>
> *Former Ruler Liu leaps Sandalwood Stream*,[37]
> *Thunder roars and destroys the Recommending Blessings stone tablet*,[38]
> *Bing Ji kills his son and sets up Xuandi*,[39]
> *Lao Lai-zi and his motley coat*,[40]
> *Academician Bao goes to Chenzhou to sell grain*,[41]
> And this play is *Mother Meng thrice moves home*.[42]

WANYAN SHOUMA. (*Sings*)
> Ever since that day, for sweet tryst with her I pray,
> I care not for fortune nor for fame;
> I can't be without her, would rather leave my home
> and with her go wandering away,

neither seeking wealth or self-advancement,
nor slaving for scholastic enhancement,
just freely relaxing in pure contentment.

  With all my heart, I'd follow her,
gladly turn strolling player.
Whatever my task, it wouldn't matter:
clowning daubed in chalk and umber,
even playing the flute or being the drummer,
or doing opening repartee or round-off patter.[?]
And I know plays, a goodly number,
acting mandarin or leading man, any role I'll master,
and of course be a flag-bearing tumbler or be a rope-dancer;
as long as I may share love's delights, the love-bird bed-quilt
    with her,
I'll barnstorm the towns and cities all,
for my living roam the wide land over.

  My heart and mind are one with yours,
I pray to be with you through the years,
never parting one moment till life disappears.

(*Dogson performs.* [*Makes gestures to warn Shouma? Or suggest he should be careful?*] *Enter Assistant Prefect Wanyan.*)

ASSISTANT PREFECT WANYAN. (*Says*)
  Even through walls there are ears,
  and does no one exist beyond your window?
I've not been into the study quarters for several days.

(*Before entering the study, he meets Dogson. Dogson performs.* [*Making gestures of warning, or of fear?*] *Golden Notice tries to dodge out of sight. Assistant Prefect Wanyan sees Golden Notice and upbraids her.*)

ASSISTANT PREFECT WANYAN. (*Sings*)
  You wretched hussy, what right have you to be in this study!
  And you, why aren't you poring over your books
      assiduously?
  And I'd hoped you'd earn scarlet robes and the golden tally!
  Little did I think you'd be such a layabout!
  What's she doing here? Quickly turn her out!
WANYAN SHOUMA.
  Father, listen to me, I beg you:
  I was sitting innocently alone in my study,
  when suddenly I saw Dogson and this girl appear;

39

and when I asked what on earth he was doing,
he told me that you had summoned her here.

GOLDEN NOTICE.

My lord, listen to me, I beg you:
The steward said you were holding a party,
he was specially fetching me here to this study;
who'd have thought – it was all a trick
to cunningly deceive me. I pray that you'll forgive me.

DOGSON.

I just tried to play the willing servant:
and now you've dragged me into trouble, you rotters, you!
Now he'll beat me till I'm numb from tip to toe,
slice off my bum and thwack my thighs in two.

ASSISTANT PREFECT WANYAN. It used to be my hope that you would
study diligently and one day become a high government official,
but now I suddenly find you behaving in such a frivolous manner
as this! Attendants!

VALET.

Lucky men, men serve,
Unlucky men serve men.

ASSISTANT PREFECT WANYAN. Hurry, go and summon the player
Wang Sishen here.

VALET. Yessir.

Heart as hasty as an arrow,
feet run as if they fly.

(*Exit valet. Enter Zhao Ruby Plum and Wang Sishen.*[43])

RUBY PLUM.

When the voice of power like thunder crashes,
one's fate is like mere dust and ashes.
I wonder what His Worship wants with us? Let's be off, then.

(*They meet Assistant Prefect Wanyan. He lectures them.*)

ASSISTANT PREFECT WANYAN. Pack your things and leave this very
night. You are forbidden to remain here any longer. First thing
tomorrow, if you are still to be seen in the vicinity, I shall set
further legal measures in motion. Now, you, old steward, this
young wretch is to be locked up here at home, and you are
forbidden to comply with any of his wishes. I shall question the
rogue at leisure tomorrow.

(*Exeunt Wanyan Shouma and Dogson. Assistant Prefect Wanyan sternly
lectures Wang Sishen and Zhao Ruby Plum.*)

ASSISTANT PREFECT WANYAN. If you fail to depart by tomorrow, I shall deal with you, taking all your past misdemeanours into account as well.

(*Exit Assistant Prefect Wanyan. Sishen and Ruby Plum discuss things.*)

SISHEN *and* RUBY PLUM.
> Nothing is decided by man's contriving:
> all one's life it is fate deciding.

(*Exeunt.*)

[Act Six]

(*Enter Dogson and Shouma.*)

WANYAN SHOUMA. (*Says*) If he can treat his own flesh and blood like this, what would he be like to strangers? Old steward, my father bullies me so cruelly, and he threw that woman of mine out last night, so what's the use of my hanging on to life? The best thing I can do is do away with myself.

DOGSON. Now then, young master, they've always said: 'A thousand days in the soil are not worth one day in the living world.' The best thing you can do is gather together some gold and silver to keep you going on the journey and go and live somewhere else for a while and follow some different living. Then, when His Worship's anger has had time to die down, you'll still be able to return. That's better than dying, isn't it?

(*Wanyan Shouma performs. [Makes gestures of despair or refutation?]*)

WANYAN SHOUMA. (*Sings*)
> I fell head over heels with Golden Notice, to her I gave my
> foolish heart,
> not dreaming my father would catch us and tear the love-bird
> pair apart.
> My beloved's gone without a trace and I'm left helpless in this
> place,
> I must put an end to this life of mine,
> yes, put an end to this life of mine.

DOGSON. (*Sings*)
> Just listen to me a while, now:
> be such a pity to do yourself in,
> but if I let you go, I fear there'll be trouble for me.
> All the same, on reflection, to lose you would be a tragedy,
> so I'll just have to share your crime and take the penalty,
> and what'll turn up, for the while wait and see,

yes, for the while just wait and see.
WANYAN SHOUMAN. For all my bitter regrets, I now have cause for
gratitude. Yes, for all my many bitter regrets, I'll now be grateful
for your kindness.

(*Exeunt.*)

[*Act Seven*]

ASSISTANT PREFECT WANYAN. (*Sings*)
If one cherishes justice in the course of duty,
in court and government one will be a celebrity,
one's staff will administer without partiality,
and the people be assured of contentment and tranquillity.

(*Says*)
If one be fair and just in everything,
need one worry what the future may bring!

(*Sends for his son.*) Attendants! Come here!

(*Enter Dogson. Performs. [Very probably telling Assistant Prefect Wanyan that
Shouma is not to be found.]*)

(*Enter man. [The Valet? More probably an imperial messenger.] Performs.
[Delivers message that the Assistant Prefect is required at court?]*)

ASSISTANT PREFECT WANYAN.
With one letter the Son of Heaven summons the world's
leading minds,
when the holy imperial edict calls, they hasten to the court.
Old steward, I don't know where my son's gone now, but I've
received the imperial summons to carry out a tour of inspection in
Honan. Make inquiries and see if you can find any news of my
son.
DOGSON. Don't worry, your worship. I'll look after things here at
home and lose no time in making inquiries about the young
master.

(*Man asks Assistant Prefect to hurry and depart.*)

ASSISTANT PREFECT WANYAN [or one of the other two?].
There'll be wine and blossoms as we go,
we'll divide our journey into two.

(*Exeunt.*)[44]

[*Act Eight*]

[GOLDEN NOTICE.]
Again and again the cuckoo urges 'Go go, go home!',
as the wanderer, in grief, must onward roam;
 the blossoms fade, the orioles grow old,
– so much wasted of youth's springtime of perfume.
Home's ten thousand miles beyond the endless misty water's
 flow,
no letters come, no word can reach me; where to look?
 where to go?
I seem nought but a lightly drifting willow-flower flake of
 snow.

(*Says*)
Over hills and through rivers toiling, trudging,
I see the evening sun westward declining,
and in the east the Jade Hare [*the moon*] rising.
The herdboy blows his flute, startling sunset ravens
 woodward fleeing,
silk wisps of mists of twilight melt, the new moon's brighter
 growing;
gazing I faintly see wondrous peaks afar, circled by dusk
 clouds enchaining,
and coldly, coldly some small river round a lonely village
 running.

SISHEN.
Ah me, the traveller's road is hard and weary,
and dusk brings further burden to his misery;
his shadow no longer shows on the desolate winding
 mountain path,
and, not knowing why, he sighs deep sighs repeatedly.

GOLDEN NOTICE.
I gaze to the sky-edge till I can gaze no more, but no old friend
 appears.
Were my heart of iron forged, yet must I still shed tears!
Piddling profit, futile fame,[45] they cause me grievous cares.

RUBY PLUM.
In the village we seek lodgings to rest the night,
and a lonely inn's bleak door comes in sight.

GOLDEN NOTICE.
Easy, you know, to sober from village wine, but how can you
 sober from sorrow?

I recall how often with my love I feasted and supped of love's
   delight;
Yet the memory of it but serves to make me sadder, that he's
   not here,
oh, who will be my comfort as I spread my lonely quilt
   tonight?

But now let's be of better cheer, not be depressed,
but steadily wend our way, be not distressed,
to hire a lodging for this night and lay us down to rest.

(*They bed down on the floor.*)

[*Act Nine*]

WANYAN SHOUMA. (*Sings*)
   I've left my home behind and along the roads I race.
   Where now in all this land does she make her dwelling place?
   More and more I sink in misery,
   chilled by my plight and lonely.
   Across rivers and over mountains I labour wearily;
   When shall I and my love-full lady, if ever again, share
      ecstasy?

(*Says*)
It's just as if I've swallowed a needle and thread:
it pricks away at my heart and tangles up my head!

(*Exit.*)

[*Act Ten*]

SISHEN. (*Says*)
   Back from business, sweat still on me,
   Back from business, sweat still on me!
When I was performing in Honan prefectural capital, Assistant
Prefect Wanyan got to know that his young son and heir Wanyan
Shouma was having a bit of (*Performs.* [*Illustrative gestures?*]) with my
daughter, and he turned us out (*Performs.* [*Acts being thrown out?*])
and told us to pack up (*Performs.* [*Does actions of packing up?*]) and go.
   A hard and unrewarding art!
   A hard and unrewarding art!

(*Exit.*)

WANYAN SHOUMA. (*Sings*)
    From parental bullying I flee across the country,
    All to be with a harlot, I hurry to and fro;
    I've pawned my coat, I've sold my horse,
    I've 'burnt my boats' and I've nowhere to go,
    I'm all alone and go back home's a thing I couldn't do;
    my little old purses are empty through and through,
    I'm broke and not a copper left in the bottom of my shoe.

    Jobless like this, lost my career,
    drifting aimless hither and thither, suffering hunger and cold
       weather,
    I come to the foot of a city-wall where willows round me
       gather,
    and cup myself some water from this ever-flowing river,
    wash my face and slick my hair to make it neater,
    add some spit to make the waves smoother, then into the city
       wander.

(*Sees shop-sign. Says*) Let's go into this tea-house and ask what's what
here. Tea-house keeper![46]

TEA-HOUSE KEEPER. (*Says*)
    With tea we welcome travellers from the Three Isles,[47]
    with our brews we see off guests from the Five Lakes.[48]

(*Meets Shouma, performs.[Asks what he wants, by gestures?]*))

WANYAN SHOUMA. (*Says*) Tell the female lead to come here, so that I
can tell her what I would like her to perform.

(*Performs.[Acts what he wants the player to perform?]*))

GOLDEN NOTICE. (*Sings*)
    Somebody's calling me over there,
    so, timidly tripping, I appear.

(*Meets Wanyan Shouma. Refuses to acknowledge him.*)

    A peasant playing play connoisseur!
    What's this ugly sight that we've got here!
WANYAN SHOUMA.
    A rat that's bitten through a calabash cane,
    – you've a very cutting jaw, young miss, 'tis plain.
GOLDEN NOTICE.
    A parrot that actually makes reply,
    – this bird dares bandy words with such as I.

WANYAN SHOUMA.

　　I'd be twice as smart as you even playing drummer!

GOLDEN NOTICE.

　　You're no match for Du Shanfu[49] in back-chat patter,
　　but you're similar to Zheng Yuanhe[50] in gear and clobber!

WANYAN SHOUMA.

　　Miss, what one spends hardly depends on the total wealth one
　　　　owns,
　　nor can one's gallantry and taste be assessed by the weight of
　　　　fine robes that one dons!

　　(Sings)
　　How can you talk like that?
　　An angel couldn't be harder to find.
　　Here am I treating you so kind,
　　and getting attacked – such a hostile mind!
　　And why've you been on the Flower Streets,
　　selling men love's treats?
　　No good, when I scold, she doesn't heed it,
　　when I tell her off, she feigns to ignore it.
　　Ah, truly it's hard to change basic nature,
　　mountains and rivers are easier to alter,
　　mountains and rivers are easier to alter.

GOLDEN NOTICE.

　　Were I a divine dragon steed,
　　I couldn't follow your wild chase from wave to wave:
　　you babble what nonsense suits you – what random rubbish
　　　　you rave!
　　You can't afford more than one dish of noodles,
　　such old tricks I can see right through;
　　but I'm not used to such almighty cheek as I'm now getting
　　　　from you.
　　Who do you think you're talking to?
　　Who do you think you're talking to?

TEA-HOUSE KEEPER.

　　Yes, come to think of it, who are you and who's she to you,
　　　　for that matter?
　　She's such a charming young lady, while you're ragged and
　　　　all of a tatter.
　　Tcha, like one of those beggars who wraps himself in a paper
　　　　sheet,
　　at the end of a daytime's scraping his living in the street,
　　gone to sleep curled up tight outside some mansion for the
　　　　night,

46

gone to sleep curled up tight outside some mansion for the
    night.
WANYAN SHOUMA.
    Spilt water is hard to retrieve,
    – at the very thought my tear-pearls flow;
    I'd hoped we would always be together,
    – who would have thought it was not to be so?
GOLDEN NOTICE.
    Pooh, let's cancel all that out,
    and to spare you any further woes,
    I'll cut my hair and offer incense
    and with you take my vows.
WANYAN SHOUMA.
    I fear in your heart, though, your words find no echo,
    I fear in your heart, though, your words find no echo.

(*Enter Sishen and Ruby Plum.*)

SISHEN. [*or Sishen and Ruby Plum together?*]. (*Says*)
    To places winging wild-geese can't attain,
    men are drawn by thoughts of fame and gain.
The theatre's just finished and the audience gone. Our daughter's
been called over to the tea-house opposite. Wonder who's there?
Let's go across.

(*They meet Wanyan Shouma. Golden Notice performs. [Introduces Shouma?]
Shouma borrows a coat. [To be warm, or to look more presentable?] He tells his
story.*)

SISHEN. All right, you want to come into my family, but I want a
zaju actor for my daughter's husband.
WANYAN SHOUMA. (*Sings*)
    So, old dramatizer, you'd have me take Liu Shuahe[51] as my
      model,
    or maybe play the youthful male[52] with charming tuneful
      throttle;
    I'll recite my patter and reel my prattle smooth as water
      pouring from a bottle.
SISHEN. (*Says*) What *zaju* can you perform then?
WANYAN SHOUMA. (*Sings*)
    I can act *Cinnabar load and floating bubbles*,[53]
    and *Great Prince Guan's single-sword meeting*;[54]
    I can perform *Guan Ning cuts the mat*.[55]
    In *Variant 'Chancellor's court'* I play Zhang Fei,[56]
    in *Thrice evading the lance* I play Yuchi Jingde.[57]
    I can act *Donkey Chen and Academician Bao in the snowstorm*,[58]

and *Undergoing interrogation Liu Cheng mistakenly deserts his wife*.[59]
Playing prime minister, I can act *Yi Yin supports Tang*,[60]
and playing the actor, I can act *Snail leading-man*.[61]

SISHEN. She's not marrying a *zaju* actor. She's only going to marry
a *yuanben* actor.

WANYAN SHOUMA. (*Sings*)
    In my acting of *yuanben*,
    I never put a foot wrong,
    and pattern myself wholly on Captain Jia. [*Some famous*
        yuanben *actor*?]
    I can caper and grimace as by nature gifted,
    I'm just made for the harlequin's chalk and umber.
    When I give a whistle,[62] the earth resounds for an age,
    I know all the *yaya xiaolailai*[63] and tomfoolery.

SISHEN. (*Says*) What *yuanben* can you act?

WANYAN SHOUMA. (*Sings*)
    And I can act *Four times not knowing*[64] and *Battling doctors*,[65]
    and I can act *Gay gallant rake*[66] and *Two get on well together*,[67]
    Huang Luzhi fights to the end,[68]
    Bright King Ma trysts in the village;[69]
    and I can act *Moving the Great Lake rocks*.[70]

SISHEN. The only man I want for my son-in-law is a writer of play-
books.

WANYAN SHOUMA. (*Sings*)
    I can add and insert[71] at great speed,
    with my writing-brush ever flying;
    I can write[72] play-books in fine clear model-script,
    the writing-clubs of the Imperial Capital[73] surpassing.

SISHEN. For my son-in-law I want a man who can play the drum
and flute.

WANYAN SHOUMA. (*Sings*)
    I can dance, I can strum, I can sing,
    the flute I can blow, the drum I can rumble;
    I can play the spirit or act the demon,
    I can box (?) and, holding a flag, I can tumble.

    Grandee's son I am, it is true,
    but, player, I'd be a good son-in-law for you.
    I can do the *Water Mother* prop-stunts,[74]
    do a *Youthful wanderings* sketch,[75] too,
    of somersaults and cartwheels take a few.[76]

SISHEN. Well, he's been a good supporter in the past and spent a
good few score taels of money on us, and what's more he's a
young gent from a good family. So I'll just take pot-luck and take

him on as my son-in-law, and work out something else later on.
Wanyan Shouma, I'll have you as my son-in-law, yes, of course I
will, it's just that I'm worried you might not manage carrying the
drums[77] and costumes.

WANYAN SHOUMA. (*Sings*)
> We'll just be strolling players, farming, labouring when
> there's opportunity,
> but if I can have this leading lady, like fish unto water I'll be,
> and humping drums won't embarrass nor carrying the
> wardrobe worry me.

SISHEN. In that case then, I'll just let him come along with us, and
work out something else later on. Ah yes, to be sure:
> Nothing's determined by man's contriving,
> all one's life it's fate deciding.

(*Exeunt.*)

[*Act Eleven*]

(A *jing*-clown, a knave, and a *chou*-clown 'suspend the stage'.[78])

WANYAN SHOUMA. (*Says*)
> At home I was a fine young squire,
> in foreign parts I'm a strolling player.

(*Performs.* [*Indicates by actions or gestures that he is weary?*])

(*Sings*)
> Weary the life of the wandering trouper and the wandering
> byways he must ply,
> and they'll never let me take a rest till we reach the rim of the
> sky!
> So here's where the young acting gent has landed – some final
> exit!

GOLDEN NOTICE. Carrying all this baggage, oh how will you bear
it?

(*Shouma recaps.* [*Tells her of his agreement with Sishen? Or of his hardships on
the journey?*])

WANYAN SHOUMA. (*Sings*)
> Strolling the cities and touring the towns,
> we wander the lakes and streams of the nation;

I'm their son-in-law, so what can I do
but bear with this shame and humiliation.

GOLDEN NOTICE.

No matter how sincere you are, you'll not convince them
whatever you say.
I'm afraid my parents will send you packing, somewhere
along the way,
and plunge myself and you, my lord, in misery and dismay.

WANYAN SHOUMA. Don't! Don't!
My tears flow forth at what you suggest.
Here's me dragging this load and my heart so depressed,
– if my old friends knew, they'd laugh fit to burst.

GOLDEN NOTICE. My own dear man,
One day we'll be proper man and wife, in the end we will, I'm
sure,
and then a fine moon will rise above our bower
and you'll never drink alone, without a 'flower'.

SISHEN.

Try and have a bit of sense, you two:
the red sun's steadily westwards sidling,
but both of you are just pointlessly dawdling.

WANYAN SHOUMA.

Please listen, I'll explain, good father:
this load's hard to bear, it's beyond my power,
your ass of a son can't walk any faster.

GOLDEN NOTICE.

Yes, that's what's holding us back, making us tarry along the
track.

RUBY PLUM.

Daughter, to reach home there's such a long long way to go.
Old husband, you're a fool not thinking what you might be
undertaking!
And you, you rotten swine, what makes you drag behind so
slow?

SISHEN.

That's enough of that now, wife!
Stop all your nagging – what's the good?
He's no enemy to make, don't go too far!
Now, you, lug the load, and press on ahead.

WANYAN SHOUMAN. (*Sings*)
One day we'll live as happy love-birds,
in the by and by we will;
but now we cannot pick and choose,
the time is not ripe still.

(Says)
Be there wine and blossoms as we go,
we'll divide our journey into two.

(Exit.)

[*Act Twelve*]

(Enter Assistant Prefect Wanyan and his page.)

ASSISTANT PREFECT WANYAN. *(Sings)*
Deep is my gratitude to the holy monarch ruling presently
that with scarlet robes and twin gold fish-tallies he has
favoured me;
Just, public-spirited, I tour the land to bring it order and
tranquillity.
My earnest prayer that it may enjoy rich harvests and times of
prosperity.
(Says) Aged of complexion and hair pure white, I occupy this
important post. Our emperor, to whom I am deeply grateful, has
conferred upon me the twin gold fish-tallies of lofty office, and, by
his blessings, I am now on a tour of inspection through the Five
Lakes and Four Seas [i.e. all over the country].
Great capacity I have indeed for rendering mandarins and
their personnel as pure as water in honesty,
and well I understand how to make the common people's
hearts as pure as ice in their common fidelity.
Page! I'm feeling bored and weary here. Go and call some play-
actors here to perform some *yuanben* to cheer me up.

*(Page calls them. Enter Wanyan Shouma and Golden Notice. Enter Sishen. He
meets Assistant Prefect Wanyan. Assistant Prefect Wanyan recaps. [Tells them
why he has summoned them?] Sishen presents the* yuanben. *Assistant Prefect
Wanyan recognizes them. Recap. [Mutual explanations of what has
happened?] He weds the couple.)*

ASSISTANT PREFECT WANYAN. *(Sings)*
Ever since my son disappeared
I've sorrowed all the time,
tears ever in my eyes, and now this surprise!
– My son has become a mummer of mime!

(Says)
Today at last that I've found you,
let us both burn incense to thank the gods above;

51

now we have met, though far from home,
may man and wife enjoy a century of perfect love.

WANYAN SHOUMA.

That day when your son stole away from home,
I travelled the vast misty water and endless mountain terrain,
lonely along the roads and grieving sorely,
till here in Dongping we're reunited once again.

GOLDEN NOTICE.

Hear me now, kind sir, please do:
that day when in the study, bent on love,
I suddenly bumped into you,
as soon as you set eyes on me there,
oh, into what a fine fury you flew!
You had me thrown out and cast us apart,
and little that day held the expectation
that we would now be man and wife.
– My thanks, dear kind sir, for your dispensation.

Qiu Hu tries to seduce his own wife

Yuan *zaju* play by Shi Junbao (1192-1276)

Characters:

OLD MRS QIU : Qiu Hu's elderly widowed mother.

QIU HU : young impoverished scholar living in the state of Lu.

SQUIRE LUO : wealthy rustic.

MRS LUO : wife of Squire Luo.

QIU PLUM-BLOSSOM BEAUTY : beautiful young wife of Qiu Hu and daughter of Squire and Mrs Luo.

MATCHMAKER : middle-aged woman who negotiates marriages.

RECRUITING SERGEANT : officer who enforces call-up orders for service in the Army.

SQUIRE LI : wealthy rustic and usurer.

ATTENDANTS of Qiu Hu.

SERVANTS : Squire Li's strong-arm thugs.

The play is set during the Zhou dynasty in the state of Lu, which existed in present-day Shantung province during the years 1207-250 BC.

Act One

(*Enter Old Mrs Qiu and Qiu Hu.*)

OLD MRS QIU.

> Flowers may bloom anew,
> but youth once gone is past recall.
> Lay no store by the glitter of gold,
> peace of mind is wealth above all.

I'm a woman from the Liu family. Since my husband passed away, I've been living all alone except for our only child, my son Qiu Hu here. But there's a wealthy local man, Squire Luo, whose daughter – called Plum-Blossom Beauty – has just married my son. The wedding took place last night, and I've arranged a spread of sweetmeats and wine today, so as to thank our in-laws with a party in the usual way. Well now, son, will you go and invite your parents-in-law round?...

QIU HU. They should be coming any moment now.

(*Enter Squire Luo and Mrs Luo.*)

SQUIRE LUO.
    Others sit pretty with half a dozen sons,
    but I've only got a daughter to my name.
MRS LUO.
    True, no dowry comes to us, but let's not spit and cuss,
    we get the in-laws' nosh-up all the same.
SQUIRE LUO. Here I am, Squire Luo, and this is my old woman. I've
a daughter called Plum-Blossom Beauty, and she's got married to
Qiu Hu. She crossed the threshold yesterday, so today the in-laws
have invited us round for drinks. We'd better be on our way there
now ... Ah, here we are at their gate. Qiu Hu! We're here!
QIU HU. Excuse me, mother, my parents-in-law are here now.
OLD MRS QIU. Invite them in, then.
QIU HU. Come in, please do.

(*Exchange of courteous greetings.*)

OLD MRS QIU. Please be seated, dears. We have wine and
sweetmeats ready for you to enjoy. Serve the wine, my son.

(*Qiu Hu hands wine to his parents-in-law.*)

QIU HU. Here you are, father-in-law and mother-in-law – bottoms-
up!
SQUIRE *and* MRS LUO. (*Drinking eagerly*) Only too delighted to taste our
new son's nuptial wine!
OLD MRS QIU. Qiu Hu, call my daughter-in-law Plum-Blossom
Beauty in here to join us.

(*Qiu Hu calls her. Enter Plum-Blossom Beauty with the wedding matchmaker.*)

PLUM-BLOSSOM BEAUTY. What do you want me for, mother-in-law?
OLD MRS QIU. Why, my dear, for you to express your thanks to your
own dear parents!
PLUM-BLOSSOM BEAUTY. Oh dear, I feel all shy and embarrassed. I
can't possibly face them.
MATCHMAKER. Come now, young lady: men and women have
been getting together and marrying since the beginning of time.
What's it to be bashful about?
PLUM-BLOSSOM BEAUTY. (*Sings*)
    When boy and girl are growing up,
    their parents teach them this:
    'When you've come of age,

54

you'll be joined in married bliss,
to honour and obey,
to give and take and to adore.'
That's what they tell us we must know ...
but they tell us nothing more!

MATCHMAKER. Well, it has come to my ears, young lady, that you've done a fair bit of book-learning, right since you was a little girl. Quite beyond me, that sort of thing. Don't your books tell you anything about the matter?

PLUM-BLOSSOM BEAUTY. (*Sings*)
They taughts us the ancient *Songs*
with moral interpretations,
which passed them off as warnings
against sinful deviations.
And then they said:
'When a lad has wooed himself a wife
and a girl has found her beau for life,
it is all
lute and dulcimer tuned in accord,
wedding-candles in the night,
springtime in the marriage bower,
as phoenixes in love delight.'

It makes me feel so awfully shy,
I wish I didn't have to go;
I dread to meet my parents' eyes
now things have happened so.
Coyly I hide my powdered face,
pretend to smooth silk skirts in place.
Oh yes, I know, I know, I know it's a woman's life
to leave her home for another as someone or other's wife,
it's a fate that most poor women meet with by and by,
but all the same I can't help feeling diffident and shy.

MATCHMAKER. You know, young lady, you really should have picked someone well off instead. Then you'd have lived a life of luxury, food galore and all the fine clothes your heart could desire. What on earth made you marry into such a down-and-out family as old Mother Qiu's?

PLUM-BLOSSOM BEAUTY. (*Sings*)
Be there cobwebs in his ovens
and his saucepans all filled with dust,
well, that's the way of my destiny,
and in him I put all my trust.
Generals and statesmen of power and celebrity

have always been produced from hovels of poverty;
and even if we both have to share
the poor man's coarse and meagre fare,
we'll only be waiting till glory's thunder
calls my dear dragon from his lair!
You see him as a nobody doomed to rot amid white-washed
    walls,
I vow he'll be a man of state who'll swagger in golden halls.
When marriage was broached, when we met, at the start,
when first I set my eyes upon him, I gave him all my heart.
Oh, a man who's not a sprout from the soil of poverty,
lacks the solid roots which can secure prosperity.

MATCHMAKER. Look now, young lady, as things stand Qiu Hu has neither money, fame nor success to his name. If you had a mind to, you know, it still wouldn't be too late to marry somebody else, someone well-to-do.

PLUM-BLOSSOM BEAUTY. (*Sings*)
Without jewels stored within our hearts,
impoverished we'll stay till life itself departs.
You tell me to wed another,
but I'll gladly first sup dearth.
What truly noble lady
was made so at her birth?
The world is full of women, but it's very well attested
no dame deserved her title while in the womb she rested.

MATCHMAKER. Go over and say hello to your parents now, young lady.

(*Plum-Blossom Beauty exchanges ceremonial greetings with her parents, then turns to her mother-in-law.*)

PLUM-BLOSSOM BEAUTY. You called for me, mother-in-law. What did you want me for?

OLD MRS QIU. I called for you to join us, dear, so that we might serve your father and mother a cup of wine.

PLUM-BLOSSOM BEAUTY. Of course. (*To matchmaker*) Bring me the wine, dear. (*She serves her parents with wine*) Dear father, dear mother, please drain the cup.

SQUIRE *and* MRS LUO. Righto! Not 'alf! Hand us the cup. There! That's the old nuptial wine down the hatch!

OLD MRS QIU. Well, Qiu Hu, now you perform your duties as host, help everybody to enjoy a nice relaxed party and let your parents-in-law enjoy some drinks at their leisure.

(*Enter Recruiting Sergeant.*)

RECRUITING SERGEANT.
> When the emperor's orders come our way,
> ours not to question why, but to obey.

I'm the Recruiting Sergeant, and I've just been instructed by my superiors to go and give Qiu Hu his army call-up orders. Ah, here I am now at Lu Clan Hamlet. Is Qiu Hu in?

(*Qiu Hu greets the Recruiting Sergeant.*)

RECRUITING SERGEANT. Qiu Hu! According to instructions received from headquarters, you are Number One on the list for National Service and I am hereby required to conscript you into the Army.

(*He places a noose round Qiu Hu's neck with which to lead him off.*)

QIU HU. Just a moment, friend. Wait till I've let my mother know.

(*Qiu Hu goes to see his mother.*)

QIU HU. There's a recruiting sergeant at the gate, mother, with my call-up orders from the government. He's come to take me away for military service!

OLD MRS QIU. Oh, my dear son, what on earth will become of us?

PLUM-BLOSSOM BEAUTY. What's all the fuss and noise about?

MATCHMAKER. They're taking your Qiu Hu away to serve in the Army.

PLUM-BLOSSOM BEAUTY. Oh, my Qiu Hu, what on earth, what on earth shall we do?

> (*Sings*) One night of love, then comes the morrow
> With the hard harsh hand of bitter sorrow!
> When he's joined the ranks, to whom shall we resort,
> two helpless women alone, deprived of our man's support?
> Take me away from these guests, far from their sight:
> how can I tell them the grief that tears me? No words seem
>   right;
> and I'm so lost in sorrow for my man that people may say
> I neglect my parents wickedly on this their special day.

MATCHMAKER. Here we are, only the Third Day of the ceremonials and still in the middle of the wedding booze, and the old recruiting sergeant turns up like a bad egg! Blow me! And here's me, lady matchmaker, hasn't had a penny bonus or a farthing in tips!

PLUM-BLOSSOM BEAUTY. (*Sings*)
> Nights unnumbered,
> while others slumbered,
> deep into the gloom
> by his blue lantern-flame

he has studied and toiled,
he has racked and moiled,
suffered, for his learning, destitution that few could bear,
endured long years of hunger on a poor man's paltry fare.
Unswerving in ambition, he's pursued his steadfast course,
towards the Palace of Jade, the Hall of the Golden Horse.
To be a minister at court was his lofty aspiration:
– to think of enlisting such a scholar into such degradation!
No other human beings get treated quite so scurvy
as these gentle humanists – the world's all topsy-turvy!
Where now that pretty saying wiseacres love to drop?
'Ability and learning will shoot you to the top!'

RECRUITING SERGEANT. Get a move on, Qiu Hu. My warrant requires the execution of my duty within a certain fixed time-limit, and I am not empowered to permit you a single day's procrastination.

QIU HU. Let me have a few minutes longer, sergeant.

PLUM-BLOSSOM BEAUTY. (*Sings*)

The brutal bumpkin, the loutish knave,
the churlish clod, all bluster and rave!
The thick-necked village ox, puffed up in his military
function –
look at him bully and bluster and bellow and brandish his
sergeant's truncheon!
A violent ruffian oaf like him, all blind duty and brawn,
why, he'd slaughter without compunction the noblest man
ever born!

OLD MRS QIU. It's only the third day of your wedding celebrations, my son, but suddenly out of the blue they come and call you up. Who's going to look after me in my old age now? Fair breaks my heart, it does!

PLUM-BLOSSOM BEAUTY. (*Sings*)

One moment ago, as the wine flowed free,
all hospitality, he took no rest
but ever bore the brimming cups
to ply each merry guest.
Yet now he is to gird a sword
and serve amid the martial horde,
to learn the soldier's skill,
to practise how to kill.
Would you say our fate is kind?
The irony rings around my mind:
only last night in blissful harmony newly wed,
with our quilt of love still lying unwarmed upon our bed;

and now it's fond farewell today
and I must wait by our wicket gate
as I send my loved one on his way.

    Where now those poets' pretty words?
'Entwined in jade-white arms,
enfolded in love's tender charms,
he lolls in the bosom of desire,
bathed in passion's lapping fire,
and traces of powder blessing his face
from his lady's soft embrace.'
Such, my love is no more true
– now there are other words for you:
'The warriors, even at rest,
never doff their burnished mail,
and all the ground has grown a skin
of myriad shiny scale on scale.'
You can be sure, whenever chaos rules the land,
liberal arts succumb and martial skills take the upper hand –
heads from shoulders tumble like boiling streams,
blood spurts from mouths and all the air is filled with
    screams.
That's where they send you now,
to war's old bestial game,
your chance, they say, to do your bit
for the nation, and to win your name.

QIU HU. My Plum-Blossom Beauty, I must leave you now and go off to do my service in the Army. You must take every care of my mother here at home, and be a loving and obedient daughter to her.

OLD MRS QIU. Go, my son, if you must. But whatever happens, always do your best to write me a letter and let me know how you're getting on!

PLUM-BLOSSOM BEAUTY. (Sings)
    The signs were right at last when marriage came our way,
in prudent fear we had steered quite clear of any unlucky day.
Bright with hope I saw reward for his ten years' sweat and
    pain –
showers of imperial favours, dew and rain to the parching
    plain.
But now
bewilderment puckers my brow:
was it then some fault of mine, that blissful fateful day of our
    marriage?

59

Did I offend the god of my star as I alighted from my
    carriage?
Did I pray with my back to the image of the progenitor of our
    clan?
Was it through some insult like that to the gods that our
    present woes began?
Already the blushing bride is cursed by a fate that sends
her husband to frontiers far away from family and friends!

    Though one have a home, no haven may be there:
truly, evil destiny tracks down the happy pair.
Are we now fated, you and I,
phoenix of love and his cooing dove,
to circle solitary till we die?
Yet you worked all the details out
to leave no earthly speck of doubt,
consulting with the wedding priest
a hundred anxious times at least.
What was it, then, what malignant power
led you to choose such an ominous hour?

OLD MRS QIU. Be on your way, my dear son, and whatever you do,
take care and be good wherever you go, and write me a letter
often, so that I don't worry about you unnecessarily.
QIU HU. I'll do everything you say, mother, dear mother. Look
after your health and take things easy while I'm away.
PLUM-BLOSSOM BEAUTY. (*Sings*)
    Rare they'll be, those winging letters that will fly
like lonely migrant geese across so vast a sky.
Far from your beloved you will lie,
only barren northern steppe-land to greet your weary eye.
And now, as tears come curtaining these stricken eyes of
    mine,
I pour you, with unsteady hand, this farewell cup of wine.
Already in my mind I am gazing over the land
to where the travel-lodges stand:
I can see the green, green willows where the verdure freshly
    spills,
the first sad stretch of river huts, the hamlets in the hills.
(*Says*) My Qiu Hu –
QIU HU. Yes, my love?
PLUM-BLOSSOM BEAUTY. (*Sings*)
    It is now no longer granted me
to press your warm body tenderly.

(Says) Last night was my first as your bride, and today you're going away to serve in the Army. *(Sings)*
> Yet our one night of married bliss
> will bear us love long after this.
> It is the prelude to the poem of pain
> that occasions the poet the greatest strain.
> And now I must be patient, conserve my grief and sorrows,
> save my tears for the dawdling dusks of a hundred grey
>   tomorrows.

(Exit with matchmaker.)

QIU HU. Father-in-law and mother-in-law, keep a kindly eye on my mother and my dear wife Plum-Blossom Beauty, for I must be off now to join the Army.
SQUIRE *and* MRS LUO. Well, that's what comes of marrying into a family of your standing. Just our daughter's bad luck! Well, on your way with you, then.

(Qiu Hu makes his ceremonial farewells.)

QIU HU. Recruiting Sergeant! I'm ready to accompany you now!
> Do not call your fate unkind, utter no curse
> that, rich in learnings, your blessings are yet so sparse,
> that, married but a few brief days,
> man and wife must part their ways.
> But apply your erudition where the games of war are played,
> and in glory you'll come home one day in brocade robes
>   arrayed.

(Exit Qiu Hu with recruiting sergeant.)

SQUIRE *and* MRS LUO. Well, Qiu Hu's off to do his bit in the Army, so we'll be off home.
OLD MRS QIU. Yes, my dears, my son has left us, so there's no point in my keeping you. I'm afraid I haven't given you a very good party.
> I'd really like to bid you stay,
> but the Army has taken my son away.
SQUIRE *and* MRS LUO.
> If he's not back in a year, don't count on his wife
> staying a grass widow all the rest of her life!

(Exit Squire and Mrs Luo.)

Act Two

(*Enter Squire Li.*)

SQUIRE LI.

> To the far-off hamlets my cornfields run,
> and in the Squire's hall it's all riotous fun;
> not like the peasant living by the toil of his shovel,
> with a jug of lukewarm vinegar wine to wet his whistle.

Squire Li, that's me. I'm rolling in wealth, with plenty of grain and fodder, land, gold and silver, and paper money. All I'm short of is a trim and trippy, pretty little wife. That's the one thing that really gets me down. I'm a big noise in this village, and all the locals are in my debt for money or grain, but they mock me all the same. 'What's the use,' they say, 'of having all that lolly without a pretty Polly?' I can't take *that* lying down! There's an old bloke in this village called Squire Luo. Used to be a wealthy fellow, with money galore, but he's got nothing left nowadays, and he's been borrowing grain from me. Still hasn't paid me back, neither! Now, he's got a daughter by the name of Plum-Blossom Beauty, a right hundred-per-cent smasher. She married a bloke called Qiu Hu, but he went off some ten years ago to do his military service and hasn't come back yet. What I'm going to do now is call that Squire Luo round here and tell him that Qiu Hu has died, and that if he'll give me his daughter to be my wife, I'll let him off his old debt of five bushels of grain, and give him some money, as a wedding gift, into the bargain. He's so hard up, he's bound to agree to the deal. I sent someone round for him a good while ago, so he should be here any moment now.

(*Enter Luo.*)

LUO.

> When a rich man beckons, so they say,
> it's a lucky star that shines your way.
> I used to be rich, as well-lined as them all,
> but it's my turn now to scurry at others' beck and call.

Yes, it's me, old Squire Luo. Must be a good ten years and more since Qiu Hu went off into the Army. Well, and here I am owing Squire Li five bushels of corn and still haven't paid him back. He's just called me round. I'm in a pretty pickle now. What on earth can I say to him if I see him, anyway? Hm, there's nobody about, so I'll go straight in. (*Greets Squire Li*) What can I do for you, then, Squire?

SQUIRE LI. Well, old fella, I've called you round because I've got a

bit of news to break to you. You know that son-in-law Qiu Hu of yours, who went off and joined the Army? Well, he's eaten too much bean-curd and died of diarrhoea.
LUO. Who told you that?
SQUIRE LI. Came to my ears, it did.
LUO. Ah, now, what am I to do about that?
SQUIRE LI. Don't upset yourself, old chap. Let me put it to you like this: your son-in-law's gone and died, but that daughter of yours is still in her prime. She won't like being a widow, will she? She won't be able to stick it. Why not marry her off to me, now?
LUO. Come off it, Squire, you can't make suggestions like that!
SQUIRE LI. If you're thinking of refusing, remember you owe me five bushels of corn. I'll have you up in court for it, and I'll get the law on your back. They'll thump the life out of you. But if you give me your daughter, I'll let you off every grain of those five bushels, and into the bargain I'll provide the usual red wedding-silk, sheep, wine and wedding-gift money. What do you say to that?
LUO. Go easy, Squire, let's not be hasty. Let's talk it over together nice and slowly and calmly. Even if I was to agree to it, I'm afraid my old woman might not.
SQUIRE LI. There are no snags. Now you just go there ahead of me, and deliver the red silk and wedding-gifts to settle with your girl's mother-in-law. You and your wife work it out between you. Once Mrs Qiu has accepted the red silk, I'll come and turn up with the sheep and wine to tie things up legally.
LUO. All right, as you say, then, Squire. You take your time, while I go on ahead and deliver the red silk. You join me later. (*Goes outside*) Huh, if I've agreed, my wife won't argue. So I'll take the red silk straight round and hand it to old Mrs Qiu.

(*Exit.*)

SQUIRE LI. Well, the old chap's given his consent, so I needn't worry about his daughter refusing to marry me. Off I go now with my presents of sheep and wine to take Plum-Blossom Beauty as my wife! And when I get her back home, I'll tip her up slap-bang, and get straight down to business. What fun! Ah, yes:
    Candle-light night in the nuptial nest,
    and the pestle tops the prizewinner's list.

(*Exit. Enter Old Mrs Qiu.*)

OLD MRS QIU. Here I am, Qiu Hu's old mother. It's a good ten years since my son went off to join the Army, and all this time I've had not a scrap of news from him. That daughter-in-law of mine has done wonders, though. I owe her so much. She does sewing, patching and laundry-work for people and keeps silkworms and harvests their cocoons, all to provide for me in my old age. It's funny, you know, but these last few days, I've been feeling rather odd. I don't know why, but my eyelids keep on flickering. It must be a sign of something in the offing. I wonder what? Never mind, I'll just sit back and take things as they come.

(*Enter Luo.*)

LUO. It's me, Squire Luo, again. Here I am at the Qius' farm. I've got it all worked out what to do when I see old Mrs Qiu. Don't need anyone to announce me, I'll march straight in. (*Greets old Mrs Qiu*) Ah, how are things with you nowadays, my dear?
OLD MRS QIU. Please take a seat, Squire. What gentle wind has blown you round here?
LUO. Well, my dear, seeing as how your dear young son and heir has been away from home so long, I thought I'd pop straight over and proffer you some good cheer to drive away your sorrows. I've got some wine here. Let me pour you a drink or two.

(*Luo serves her the customary three cups of wine drunk by parents in legal token of acceptance of a marriage offer. She drinks unawares.*)

LUO. That's it, my dear. And now you've downed the wine, I've also got a piece of red satin here, for my daughter to make herself a dress out of.
OLD MRS QIU. Oh, you shouldn't! It's too kind of you. When Qiu Hu comes back home, I'll send him round to thank you properly for being so generous.
LUO. Done, done, done!
OLD MRS QIU. What do you mean, 'Done, done, done'?
LUO. I mean, you've been done and my trick's worked, my dear! That wine and red silk didn't come from me, they both came from our local nob, Squire Li. Those three goblets of wine that you drank just now were the wine of marriage-consent, and this here silk's the red betrothal silk. Your Qiu Hu has died, and Squire Li wants to make Plum-Blossom Beauty his wife. He'll be round here in person soon, bringing a sheep and more wine. Well, I'm off home. Cheerio.
　　　It's all Squire Li's cunning game,
　　　but you took his gifts – you're to blame!
　　　Best give him our daughter to be his wife,
　　　if you don't want a court case and the scandal of your life.

(*Exit.*)

OLD MRS QIU. The wicked old fellow! Well, now he's run off, how can I face my daughter-in-law and break the news to her? Where are you, daughter-in-law?

(*Enter Plum-Blossom Beauty.*)

PLUM-BLOSSOM BEAUTY. It's me, Plum-Blossom Beauty. Since Qiu Hu left me, ten years have crept by. I fetch and carry for other people so as to earn my mother-in-law's keep. She hasn't been feeling quite right these last few days. I've just finished my work in the silkworm sheds, so I think I'll go and see how she is. Oh, my Qiu Hu, when will you come home to me? (*Sings*)

Since we shared in love one brief ecstatic night,
I've sent a million sighs winging their futile flight.
What irony that gossips, earnest for all their jesting tone,
once foresaw us surely bound for a future as Darby and Joan!
Now I'm left with his aged mother, who's in an ailing way,
and mostly keeps to her bed day after dragging day.

(*Says*) Some folks say, 'Why, Plum-Blossom Beauty! Get a doctor to come round and see that mother-in-law of yours.' Oh so right, so very right of them! (*Sings*)

I *ought* to call a doctor to see if her pulse sounds funny,
but I don't know how to mix that medicine called money.
And in this village the only doctors you ever see
are pedlars of pure rubbish, quacks of the first degree.
These days I've prayed and prayed, all heaven and earth
    implored,
that she may see her son again and their happiness be
    restored.
There's a very common saying that I've often heard before
that you should never set much store on your daughter-in-
    law
– she's as easy to replace as plaster on the wall,
and usually she's hardly worth anything at all.
Yet, white-haired mother of my man, with all my heart I
    yearn
that better times may bless you and your good health soon
    return.
Heaven on High!
When will that dear man of mine
home once more his steps incline?
Of where he is and how he fares
there's been no news in all these aching years.

(*Greets Old Mrs Qiu. Says*) Won't you eat a little rice-gruel, my dear mother-in-law?

OLD MRS QIU. There's one little thing I've been meaning to tell you, daughter-in-law. I know Qiu Hu isn't at home now, but you're still a young girl and it wouldn't do any harm for you to spruce yourself up a bit, make yourself look a bit better combed. When the pedlar calls at the house, buy a little rouge and powder to make your face up. And dress yourself a bit smarter. The way you go about, with your hair all straggly and smuts on your face, you'll make a laughing-stock of yourself.

PLUM-BLOSSOM BEAUTY. (*Sings*)

> My mother-in-law declares
> I should mend my dowdy airs,
> I should not go around
> looking such an awful mess,
> a young girl should look pretty;
> I must wear another dress,
> I'm a fright, I look a sight,
> I've no sense of what is right.

(*Says, as part of song*) Oh, my Qiu Hu! (*Sings*)

> He's been gone for years and years,
> ten thousand hills and rivers lie between us,
> and, his mother and wife, we struggle alone,
> with no one to protect or to maintain us!

OLD MRS QIU. Keep calm, daughter-in-law. You're getting in a temper fit to smash house and home to bits.

PLUM-BLOSSOM BEAUTY. (*Sings*)

> Don't be afraid that I'd make the blunder
> of smashing house and home asunder,
> for we couldn't scrape tupporth of fish-glue then
> to try and stick it together again.

(*Says*) So my dearest mother-in-law, you think that when the pedlar comes to the house, I should buy some rouge and powder and put some make-up on my face. Well, let me tell you something: Qiu Hu has been gone for ten years, and we've got nothing to wear and nothing to eat, and, dear mother-in-law, (*Sings*)

> We're so poor we couldn't raise the cash
> to mend a broken riddle-mesh!

(*Enter Squire Li with Luo and Mrs Luo, followed by a noisy band of musicians in wedding array.*)

SQUIRE LI. Off I go to bag myself a wife.

> Candle-light night in the nuptial nest
> and the pestle tops the prizewinner's list.

PLUM-BLOSSOM BEAUTY. There's such a noise of pipes and drums right outside, mother-in-law. Can it be people celebrating the Ox King Festival? I'll just go and take a look.

OLD MRS QIU. Yes, why don't you, my dear?

PLUM-BLOSSOM BEAUTY. Why, it's Mummy and Daddy! What's brought you here?

LUO. We're bringing you a husband we've found for you.

PLUM-BLOSSOM BEAUTY. What's that, Daddy? A husband? Who for?

LUO. For you.

PLUM-BLOSSOM BEAUTY. How can you say such a thing! You've found a husband for me? (Sings)

> You turn up here with mutton and wine
> and a gang of musicians, and think everything's fine!
> I have a husband of my own, why find me another spouse?
> Just like you, you peasant oaf, to have so little tact or nous!

LUO. Qiu Hu has died, daughter. Now Squire Li *himself* wants to make you his wife.

PLUM-BLOSSOM BEAUTY. (Sings)

> Once wife to Tom, I shall never marry
> any other Dick or Harry.
> How can you entertain such thoughts?
> How can you be so dense?
> Have another little think,
> try and use some common sense.

MRS LUO. Now then, daughter, you know what they say: 'The greatest virtue in a child is obedience to its parents' words.' Just you marry him now without any further fuss or ado.

PLUM-BLOSSOM BEAUTY. (Sings)

> 'Wed a cock, remain his faithful hen'.
> My parents fixed my first marriage,
> and those were their instructions then,
> and I undertook in glad sincerity
> to share my husband's lot, be it wealth or poverty.
> From early morning till night the luxury
> of hulled white rice is never granted me,
> nor all these years was I ever blessed
> to be fed enough or amply dressed.
> I've withstood the heart of winter,
> shivering through the icy weather,
> borne up through pangs of hunger,
> held house and home together,
> and, banish the thought, never swerved or fallen short.

LUO. Stop all this blethering fuss! – Your mother-in-law has accepted the red wedding-silk.

PLUM-BLOSSOM BEAUTY. Oh has she? I'll just go and see about that! (Goes to Old Mrs Qiu.) Dearest mother-in-law, to think how ever since

67

Qiu Hu went away, all these ten years, I've been slaving away,
fetching and carrying for other people so that I could support you.
How *could* you go and marry me to another man? What's my life
worth now? I'd best put an end to it.

OLD MRS QIU. It wasn't my fault at all, dear daughter-in-law. Your
father foisted the silk on me. It was him, he sold you.

(*She weeps.*)

PLUM-BLOSSOM BEAUTY. (*Sings*)
　　She weeps and wails, sore distressed,
　　and sorrow assails my troubled breast.

(*Goes outside. Sings*)

　　Father, don't you care, have you so thick a skin
　　as to ignore the scorn of friends and kith and kin?

LUO. Hold on, now, I fully intend to give your mother-in-law her
fair share of the wedding gifts!

PLUM-BLOSSOM BEAUTY. (*Sings*)
　　How kind!
　　So it's sharing out the wedding spoils that's on your mind!

LUO. Come on now, dear girl. You marry him and I'll come in for
a bite of meat and a spot of booze from him.

PLUM-BLOSSOM BEAUTY. (*Sings*)
　　Poor daddy mine,
　　it must be your first chance of snacks and wine!

MRS LUO. Now then, daughter, you'll get a wedding party, too.
We'll take care of that.

PLUM-BLOSSOM BEAUTY. (*Sings*)
　　Oh mummy, you sweety,
　　you do so love to throw a party!

SQUIRE LI. Hey, not so much of the chit-chat, young lady! Take a
gander at me. Not bad-looking, eh? (*Puts on a grotesque, would-be-
seductive expression. Receives a flurry of clouts from Plum-Blossom Beauty.*)

PLUM-BLOSSOM BEAUTY. (*Sings*)
　　Here's a box round the ears to put you in your place,
　　Come a step nearer, and I'll scratch your face.

(*Says*) Such wild indecency in an orderly peacetime society! (*Sings*)
　　What a cheek you've got to accost ladies like that!

(*Goes inside to Old Mrs Qiu. Sings*)
　　Ah me, dear mother-in-law, now I see,
　　you were helpless, they tricked you so cruelly.

LUO. What's all the argy-bargy for? You disobedient, pig-headed
little bitch!

PLUM-BLOSSOM BEAUTY. (*Sings*)
 I'm disobedient and awkward, they tell me,
 for not letting my mummy and daddy sell me.
 Oh, daddy mine, and all this while
 I never guessed you could be so vile!
SQUIRE LI. Hey there, young lady, stop making a shindy. It's no
insult that I'm offering you. You know the old saying, I'm sure:
 For a phoenix only a phoenix is a fitting mate,
 and a love-bird cock needs a love-bird hen to share his love-
  dove fate.
PLUM-BLOSSOM BEAUTY. (*Sings*)
 So a phoenix needs a phoenix for his mate,
 and a love-bird needs another to share its fate?
 Well, here's a proverb that's more suitable for you:
 'A clod should walk with a clodhopper's gait!'

(*The musicians play some wedding music, much to Plum-Blossom Beauty's anger. She sings*)

 Keep your bumpkin drums
 to entertain your clodpole chums!
SQUIRE LI. Come on, come a bit closer, young lady. I tell you,
there's no one in the whole village with money like mine.
PLUM-BLOSSOM BEAUTY. (*Sings*)
 As a matter of fact, I don't care for your money,
 with me it cuts no dash;
 why don't you, since you praise your wealth,
 just snuggle in bed with all your cash?
LUO. Watch it, you young hussy! You'd be far better off marrying
Squire Li than living this poverty-stricken life here. Enjoy some
real good living you would, then.
PLUM-BLOSSOM BEAUTY. (*Sings*)
 My dear Papa, to make me this fellow's wife
 you would 'lure' me to his bed at the point of a knife.
SQUIRE LI. But I'm a handsome-looking chap and no mistake!
PLUM-BLOSSOM BEAUTY. (*Sings*)
 To me you have the face to grace some public-execution
  place,
 your kith and kin are all yokel slobs,
 your friends all bumpkin local nobs,
 ignorant lumpkin lout of no rank or name or note!

 But my own dear man, beneath some other sun
 who knows what glories he may now have won?
 Perhaps he is riding

a jet-capped coach that's broidery-draped and has patterned
    wheels,
or a noble horse with a saddle of gold and a harness set with
    jewels,
with two files of footmen, spick and span as they hold
pitchers and silver bowls, insignia of his rank,
his ladle-large seal of office, shining gold, by his flank,
and, big as a door-curtain, his Field-Marshal's flag waving
    bold.

And recalling that his mother is seventy this year
he'll return where he was born and bred, he'll very soon be
    here,
and when he's safely back with his loving wife and mother,
I'll not forget my vengenance, looby donkey brother!
And on that day, who shall say him nay?
– his tiger-wolf lictors will seize you suddenly.
(*Says*) Then he'll ask, 'Who's been trying to seduce my wife? Who's
been bullying my mother?' (*Knocks Squire Li flat. Sings*)
    I assure you that you won't get off scot-free!

(*Exit Plum-Blossom Beauty with Old Mrs Qiu.*)

SQUIRE LI. Hey, what does she mean by it? Nagging at me and
flattening me, and she isn't even my wife yet! You'll hear more of
me, I can tell you!
    I was licking my lips for the wedding night,
    but I got a proper bashing from the aim of my desires.
LUO *and* MRS LUO.
    It's your own bad luck, Squire, that's what's got you down,
    don't blame our daughter with her hoity-toity airs.

(*Exeunt all together.*)

Act Three

(*Enter Qiu Hu in fine robes of high rank and office.*)
QIU HU. Here I am: Qiu Hu. After I was called up into the Army, I
came to the notice of the Commander-in-chief, who considered
me a fine warrior, admired my liberal erudition and was
altogether delighted with me. And in view of various outstanding
services I rendered under his banner I have by now been
promoted to the post of Minister of the Exterior. But I submitted
that I had been away from home for ten years, neglecting my aged

mother all that time, and petitioned for leave to return, and our ruler, the Duke of Lu, has indeed been so kind as to present me with an ingot of gold to take home to provide for my mother's welfare. So now, in glory and clad in robes of brocade, I'm going home to see my mother once more.

> Amid tears and wailing I went off to join the troops,
> now smiling and in glory I return towards my house,
> bearing glittering gold for my own dear mother
> and comfort and affection for my dainty young spouse.

(*Exit.*)

(*Enter Old Mrs Qiu.*)

OLD MRS QIU. I'm Qiu Hu's old mother. There's been no news from him since he left us. And the other day we had a terrible row with the in-laws. It was a good thing my daughter-in-law was so virtuous and refused to marry again. Otherwise, who on earth would there have been to look after me? Today she's already gone out to pick mulberry-leaves in the mulberry grove, for feeding the silkworms. She *does* work hard, and all for my sake. I only hope I may be her daughter-in-law in our next incarnation so that I can repay her kindness. Oh, it's muggy today! Makes me feel all sleepy. I think I'll go and have a rest.

(*Exit.*)

(*Enter Plum-Blossom Beauty carrying a basket for the mulberry leaves.*)

PLUM-BLOSSOM BEAUTY. Off I go to pick some mulberry leaves. (*Sings*)
> Since first I wed, living's always been a feat,
> we've never been able to make ends meet.
> My horoscope maybe fixed this loneliness on me,
> this hunger, cold and toil that nearly slay me,
> and then my own parents abuse and betray me!
> And with living already hard enough and spirits low,
> along come wretched harvests to add further to our woe!

> All we see is cloud-filled sky above the wild woods,
> which we foolishly took as summer rain for our fields.
> Who made the Lord on high visit us with this blight?
> Angered him to punish us peasants with this bitter plight?
> Ah misery – I loved my man in a million ways,
> but cuddled with him for only one night,
> before that partner of mine for life
> was whisked out of my sight.

Let me lay my wicker basket on the ground
and pick fresh mulberry-leaves from all around ...
lush foliage granting heavy shade ...
a blur of kingfisher-green brocade ...
Under the leaves with their verdant mist
I part a way and rustle through,
brushing the branches as I weave
and scattering twig-tip dew.

Here I am a farming wife,
my job to tend the silk cocoon –
plucking, picking, like some wanton
singing-girl beneath the moon!
Must hurry now, for the silkworms
must not miss their sup,
no matter if the leaves get torn
and the twigs all twisted up.

(*Says*) I've suddenly come hot all over. I'll take off my dress and let it air in the sun. (*Takes off dress and lays it to air in the sun. Enter Qiu Hu, who has meanwhile changed into his ordinary clothes.*)

QIU HU. Here I am: Qiu Hu. I'm not far from home, and I've just changed into my ordinary clothes for a bit. Why, there's our mulberry-groves. Those mulberry-trees have all put on quite a bit of height. Let's take a closer look. Hm, why is the gate to the grove open? Let's have a look inside. (*Sees Plum-Blossom Beauty, whom he fails to recognize after all these years*) Mmm! Now there's a nice bit of stuff! She's standing with her back to me, so I can't see her face, but the back of her's nice enough, with that pure white neck and raven hair of hers! How can I get her to tu⸛ ⸛ round? I certainly wouldn't mind having a proper look at her! Ah, I know. I'll tickle her fancy with a little quatrain. That's bound to turn her head.

Who is the maiden of sweet fifteen,
with her basket, on mulberry-leaves intent?
Whose silken dress blows from a branch
and fills the whole grove with her heavenly scent?

(*Says*) H'm, that's strange. Can't she hear me? Impossible! Let me recite it once more. (*Recites the quatrain once more.*)

(*Plum-Blossom Beauty turns round to get her dress and sees him.*)

PLUM-BLOSSOM BEAUTY. Who on earth can that be coming here when I'm picking mulberry-leaves? What does he think he's doing, coming into our grove? I'll put my dress on. Oh dear, too late, too late!

(*Qiu Hu bows to her.*)

QIU HU. My respects to you, young lady.

(Plum-Blossom Beauty, very flustered, returns his ceremonious greeting.)

PLUM-BLOSSOM BEAUTY. *(Sings)*
 In a flurry and fluster I answer, 'Good-day, Master'.
QIU HU. You honour me too much, young lady.
PLUM-BLOSSOM BEAUTY. *(Sings)*
 This man is no vagabond rake in quest of some lewd game,
 but surely some learned graduate, a gentle scholar of good
  fame.
 See how he bows with such courtesy,
 how nicely clasps his hands and addresses me!
 Sir, you must have read the classics, be steeped in Confucian
  ethics –
QIU HU. Would you be so good as to provide some cool liquid
refreshment for me, young lady?
PLUM-BLOSSOM BEAUTY. *(Sings)*
 I'm a gentle lady of the sericulture trade,
 not here to fetch you food like some labouring maid.
QIU HU. There's no one else about, young lady. Come closer. Be
my wife, eh? Nothing to be afraid of, is there, now?
PLUM-BLOSSOM BEAUTY. *(Furious. Sings)*
 Suddenly assailing one with foul and sly suggestions!
 I mistook you for a decent human being,
 and now you behave in such a vulgar way –
 what on earth do you imagine that you're doing?
QIU HU. Come on now, my dear! There's nobody else around. I
beg and beseech you.
 Don't toil the soil when you can till with a young lad,
 don't pick mulberry when there's a gent for you to wed.
Come on now. Let me, won't you?
PLUM-BLOSSOM BEAUTY. You immoral beast! *(Sings)*
 You want me to be your loving bird,
 I'll be a goatsucker – haven't you heard
 its sad cooing call, all it seems to say
 is, 'Hurry, hurry, be on your way'!
QIU HU. But surely you're a sweet sericultural maid, not a
disagreeable goatsucker bird?
PLUM-BLOSSOM BEAUTY. *(Sings)*
 But you would have me neglect my trade
 and give my attentions to you instead;
 but should my silkworms fade and die,
 then how on earth would I get by?

QIU HU. (*Aside*) This is getting us nowhere. Action is called for. (*Grabs hold of Plum-Blossom Beauty*) Come on, young lady, let me.
PLUM-BLOSSOM BEAUTY. (*Pushes him away*) Keep away from me! (*Sings*)

>Who are you, you common lout,
>brazenly mauling me about,
>with swimming, glaring, maddened eyes,
>and clawing me with clutching paws?

QIU HU. Even if you could fly, you'd never get past that gate!
PLUM-BLOSSOM BEAUTY. (*Sings*)

>He blocks my road home and leaves me no choice
>but to scream for help at the top of my voice.

(*Shouts*) Pedlar Ma, Cowhand Wang, Zhang the Shepherd! Come quickly!
QIU HU. Don't shout, young lady!
PLUM-BLOSSOM BEAUTY. (*Sings*)

>He seeks to force me in this grove to gratify his appetite,
>I'm all of a-tremble tip to toe, he puts me in such a fright.
>He hugs me, seeking to caress,
>tugs me, drags me by my dress,
>dodges to and fro and will not let me go.
>To think I first mistook him for some high celebrity!
>Now I see the thug he is, all ignorant brutality!

QIU HU. (*Aside*) Just a moment, lad. This girl's not going to give in, so what the devil can I do now? Ah, I've got that ingot of gold on me. The Duke of Lu gave me it for my mother's upkeep, but my mother knows nothing of that. What's the old saying? – 'Money moves the heart'. I'll hand the girl this ingot of gold. It's bound to make her drop her defences and see eye to eye with me. (*Takes out the gold and goes up to Plum-Blossom Beauty again*) Look now, young lady, if you'll agree to be mine, I'll give you this ingot of gold.
PLUM-BLOSSOM BEAUTY. (*Aside*) The wicked whoreson! Well, now he's produced his ingot of gold, it's given me an idea. Hey, you, why couldn't you have told me before that you had an ingot of gold? Let's just look and make sure nobody's coming first. You look over there, and I'll look over this way.
QIU HU. She's given in. Yes, you go and look over there.
PLUM-BLOSSOM BEAUTY. (*Slips out through the gate*) Just listen to me, you filthy beast! Don't you know the proverb:

>At the sight of gold a man's morals dissolve,
>but gold doesn't weaken a girl's chaste resolve?

When you see a girl won't do as you please, you bring out your gold, your filthy beast. You think gold has all that effect, do you? (*Sings*)

They say, 'There are jade-fair maidens found in books',
    meaning culture is the way to win a wife of winsome looks.
QIU HU. Pah! I've let her pull a fast one on me!
PLUM-BLOSSOM BEAUTY. (*Sings*)
    You dangle your gold to buy yourself sex,
    but good men strew gold to garner good books!
    Ugh! You wealthy young playboys, always flashing gems,
    and banking on the power of the paper in your purse!
    Did they never tell you, by your money one can smell you,
    judge you by your spending, for better or for worse?
    You make me furious,
    you ape in human cap and cape!
    you goat in human hat and coat!
QIU HU. If you won't have me now, young lady, how about my going home with you and arranging a proper marriage?
PLUM-BLOSSOM BEAUTY. (*Sings*)
    Would you seek your blissful match
    beneath our cowshed thatch?
    If you're after a phoenix you'd do best
    not to look for one in our poor crow's nest.
    Our silk-cocoon paper is not the stuff
    for marriage lines, it's somewhat rough;
    the mulberry saplings of our grove
    grow into no branch-twined trees of love;
    the twin-eyed fish of love would choke
    in our steeping-pools where the hemp-strands soak;
    and the windlass of our well would never raise to light
    those joined jade-ring symbols of love's ardour bright!
    And I'm certain, wretch, that one of these days
    you'll be struck down dead for your wicked ways!
    QIU HU. Mind what you're saying, miss. If you still refuse, I
      might as well round off what I've started by spanking the
      daylights out of you!
PLUM-BLOSSOM BEAUTY. Who are you threatening to spank?
QIU HU. You!
PLUM-BLOSSOM BEAUTY. (*Sings*)
    Just so much as glance at me,
    and I'll brand your ugly pate!
    Just so much as tug at me,
    and I'll lop off your hands and feet!
    Just touch me once, just do,
    and I'll flog your thigh-bones in two!
    Pinch me but once and you'll rue it sore,
    you'll find yourself transported a thousand miles or more!

Just put your arms around me, and like doomed men from
    their jails,
you'll be heading for the crossroads on a hurdle spiked with
    nails!
Yes, and then I'll finish you off with ten thousand slices!
And don't imagine that suffices –
I wouldn't have yet begun
to wreck your family tombs and annihilate your clan!

QIU HU. What a wicked woman! All right, you turn me down, but
why do you have to say all those nasty things to me?

PLUM-BLOSSOM BEAUTY. (*Picks up her basket of mulberry leaves. Sings*)
The ruffian stands all boggle-eyed
that I should subject the dead to shame;
all covered in mortification
that I should profane his forebears' name!
Who asked you into our mulberry grove
to seduce the wife of a respectable man?
– I'll dig out your ancestors, seven ages back,
and just try and stop me if you can!

(*Exit.*)

QIU HU. What a telling-off I got from her! Well, I'll take this ingot
of gold and go back home and look after my old mother with it.
    When I set eyes on that exquisite bit of stuff,
    I fell in love, I lost all track.
    I tried to seduce her, but couldn't induce her,
    and she threatened my forebears seven ages back.

(*Exit.*)

Act Four

(*Enter Old Mrs Qiu.*)

OLD MRS QIU.
    Out with the sun to pluck and pull,
    at noon the mulberry-basket is still not full;
    now you realize the satined ladies and their ilk
    have never been the women who produced the silk.
Here I am: Qiu Hu's mother. My daughter-in-law went off to pick
some mulberry leaves. Why isn't she back by now?

(*Enter Qiu Hu in all his fine official robes and accompanied by his attendants.*)

QIU HU. It's me: Qiu Hu. Here I am, right at the gate of my own home. I must go in at once. Dear mother, your son has returned to you.

OLD MRS QIU. (*In alarm*) Who are you, my good lord?

QIU HU. None other than your own son. I'm Qiu Hu.

OLD MRS QIU. Oh, my dear son, you're a mandarin now! Oh, I've been longing for you dreadfully!

QIU HU. (*Giving her the gold*) Yes, mother, I'm a mandarin now, and I hold the the post of Minister of the Exterior. The Duke of Lu has sent me home in brocade robes and bestowed this ingot of gold upon me so that I might keep you in the style you deserve.

OLD MRS QIU. Ah yes, my son, these past few years have been bitter and hard, and no mistaking.

QIU HU. Where has my Plum-Blossom Beauty gone, mother?

OLD MRS QIU. (*Very sadly*) Oh, my son, but for my daughter-in-law looking after me all these ten years you've been away, I'd have died of starvation long ago. She's gone to the mulberry-grove to pick some mulberry-leaves.

QIU HU. Where did you say she'd gone, mother?

OLD MRS QIU. She's gone to pick some mulberry-leaves. She should be back any moment now.

QIU HU. Phew! Could that girl I tried to seduce in the mulberry-grove just now have been my own wife? Well, I think I know what to do when she comes back.

(*Enter Plum-Blossom Beauty in a panic.*)

PLUM-BLOSSOM BEAUTY. Run, run, run! (*Sings*)

But for the reason that June's the busiest month of the season,
so much farming work to do,
I'd have grabbed that lout, he deserves a mighty clout,
and I wouldn't have lightly let him go!
But I worried about the roosting crows and the darkening of
the sky,
anxious lest my silkworms fade while my leaves all withered
dry.
Everywhere I look, the gentle mulberry,
farmsteads and forests are all that I can see;
I hope no neighbours catch a glimpse of me
in such an awful stew – what would I do?

(*Says*) H'm, we're not mayors or squires, so what's that horse doing tethered outside our house? I'll just put this basket of mulberry-leaves in the silkworm shed. Now I'll take a peep. Why, the wicked whoreson! He tries to seduce me in the mulberry-grove, and when I won't give in, he openly chases me to my home! (*Sings*)

He thinks he can bully us, push us around,
the cheeky ruffian, and on our own ground!
It makes me choke with anger;
I lift my skirts and in I race,
march right up to him and without ado
grab him by his satin robe and tell him to his face:
'We'll clearly have to go to court to settle things with you!'

(*Seizes hold of Qiu Hu.*)

OLD MRS QIU. Don't pull him about, daughter-in-law. It's Qiu Hu come home.

PLUM-BLOSSOM BEAUTY. (*Lets go of him. Sings*)
Well, well, just like Zeng Can, the virtuous son in the story,
come back to Mummy in brocade robes and covered all over
in glory!

(*Goes outside and calls Qiu Hu out to her.*) Qiu Hu, come here!

QIU HU. What do you want me out here for, my Plum-Blossom Beauty?

PLUM-BLOSSOM BEAUTY. Have you by any chance been trying to have an affair with some young girl?

QIU HU. (*Aside*) That's done it! I'll just have to play it this way. – As if I'd ever have flirted with another girl, my dear Plum-Blossom Beauty. When did I?

PLUM-BLOSSOM BEAUTY. (*Sings*)
How is it your heart connives at seducing others' wives,
seeking kisses from another man's missus?
Such sottish impudicity and libertine lubricity!
Do you think your conduct suits
that ivory emblem of rank you hold,
your purple sash, your seal of gold, your black court-boots?
So you have won yourself splendour and lofty reputation,
and occupy the station of pillar of our nation!

(*Says, as part of song*) But how do you think I've managed to support your mother this last ten years? (*Sings*)
What humiliation for the wife you wed in youth,
in those poor inglorious years!
All the lonely pain she's borne,
her heart with sorrow torn and eyes wept dry of tears!
Little did I know that the love of one night-time
was the prelude for harsh solitude for what seemed half a
lifetime!

OLD MRS QIU. Daughter-in-law, come in here.

(*Plum-Blossom Beauty and Qiu Hu go in to Mrs Qiu.*)

OLD MRS QIU. Just look, daughter-in-law, the Duke of Lu has sent me this ingot of gold to provide for me in my old age. I owe so much to you for all you've done for me these past ten years that I'm going to give you this gold as a sign of my gratitude. Take it now.

PLUM-BLOSSOM BEAUTY. I couldn't think of accepting it, dear mother-in-law. You keep it to make gold hairpins for your hair. (*Goes outside and calls*) Qiu Hu, come out here.

QIU HU. What do you want me for now?

PLUM-BLOSSOM BEAUTY. (*Sings*)

> You play the thief, but here's the snag,
> I can pin it on you, I've got the swag!
> You flimsy crystal tower, don't try and bluster:
> the Duke of Lu gave this gold to his minister ...
> for you to bring back here and support your mother dear!

(*Says*) But what if you were to offer this gold to someone outside the family, a girl? Why, (*Sings*)

> If she'd accept your gold and comply,
> brilliant lordling, you wouldn't be concerned
> that your own dear mother might go hungry and die.
> Ah, when joy comes on the soul
> the streams of genius start to roll:
> you must recall one of the *Odes*, a little thing
> with a verse on 'A maid love-yearning in spring',
> (and how the 'seductive knight solved her plight'!)
> And the other one, let's consider its lines
> and ponder their meaning for me and you:
> 'Come to a tryst amid the mulberry-trees,
>   down by the river we'll *rendez-vous*.'

(*Says*) Dear Qiu Hu, are you sure you haven't been trying of late to have an affair with some woman or other?

QIU HU. Oh, you're so suspicious!

PLUM-BLOSSOM BEAUTY. (*Sings*)

> Have you slept?
> Did the pretty maid accept?

(*Picks up basket for mulberry leaves. Sings*)

> Enough! I take my basket so
> and off to pick mulberry-leaves I go.
> No good blaming my parents for their choice of match:
> on the surface so imposing, inside not up to scratch.
> One night of wedding candles and wedded bliss,
> who'd have thought the outcome would be like this!

Love-bird, seek another partner for your golden bower;
wealthy lord, I relinquish new fortune's pretty flower,
and hungry shall daily haunt the highways of the town,
begging scraps of rice, and cold water to wash it down.
Now give me a scrap of paper, though,
one little piece that will let me go!

QIU HU. A certificate of divorce? Why do you ask for that?

PLUM-BLOSSOM BEAUTY. (*Sings*)
The case is all too clear,
let others the explicit verdict cast:
'A man strives after wisdom,' it's said,
but 'A girl hugs her virtue to the last.'

OLD MRS QIU. What's all that quarrelling about, Qiu Hu?

QIU HU. Plum-Blossom Beauty spurns me, mother.

OLD MRS QIU. Why on earth do you do that, daughter-in-law?

PLUM-BLOSSOM BEAUTY. Just listen to me, Qiu Hu:
My virtue as flawless as pure ice,
I refused the gold you proffered me;
Had I smiled and given in, would you ever have believed
that all these years I'd kept my chastity?

Hand me a certificate of divorce, Qiu Hu. Give me a divorce!

QIU HU. My Plum-Blossom Beauty, you're making such a mistake.
I've brought you finely inscribed deeds bestowing upon you the
titles of a noble lady, as, being my wife, you now are by right. I've
brought you a lofty carriage drawn by a team of four horses. You
are now to be a Dame of the Shire. How on earth can you think of
demanding a divorce and leaving me?

PLUM-BLOSSOM BEAUTY. (*Sings*)
Do you think I'd touch those gorgeous titles?
Or even glance at the rose-hued cloak and golden hat?
(*Says, as part of song*) Even if I had them, (*Sings*)
I'd lock them securely in a cupboard,
I'd never dare to wear anything like that!

Phew! Now what's the wind blown along,
'filling the garden with its fragrant' ... pong!?

(*Enter Squire Li, Luo, Mrs Luo and servants.*)

SQUIRE LI. They accepted my red wedding-silk, and then the girl
had the cheek to give me a lashing with her tongue. Well, don't
think I give up as easily as that! This time I've brought a gang of
strong-arm lackeys with me, and I'm going to carry her off by
force!

LUO *and* MRS LUO. Yes, today seems a good wedding-day by the

horoscope, so we'll come along and help you abduct the hussy.
(*They see Plum-Blossom Beauty*) Why, there's our daughter Plum-
Blossom Beauty, isn't it?
PLUM-BLOSSOM BEAUTY. (*Sings*)
> Here they come to add frost to the snow!
> I've already spurned this statesman, this 'fisher of mighty
>   fish';
> so you, you herder of common cows,
> you'd best abandon your lustful wish!

QIU HU. (*Bellows*) Hey you, fellow! What do you think you're doing,
marching into my house?
SQUIRE LI. (*In alarm*) Cor, he's a mandarin now! He's not just a
soldier any more! – Ahem, I heard of your return home in
'brocade robes and glory', so I came round specially to offer my
congratulations.
LUO *and* MRS LUO. Pah! So that's it. You told us he'd died!
SQUIRE LI. It's not him that's died – it's me!
QIU HU. So! The rogue has been fabricating rumours with intent to
deceive and trying to make off with the wife of another man by
force. Attendants! Arrest him and escort him to Juye County
Court, where he shall be tried and sentenced to a very stiff
punishment.

(*Attendants seize Squire Li and place him in bonds.*)

SQUIRE LI. It wasn't my idea. It was your parents-in-law. They
owed me five bushels of grain and sold me their daughter to repay
their debt.
QIU HU. If that's the case, it merely adds to the dastardliness of your
crimes. Clearly you've been practising illegal and criminally
inflated usury and coercing people to sell their daughters.
Attendants, inform the county magistrate that he is to be heavily
punished, that he is to receive forty strokes of the rod, to be
exposed in public in a cangue for three months, and to be fined
two hundred and fifty bushels of grain, which are to be used for
the relief of the poor and needy. On no account is he to be let off
lightly!
ATTENDANTS. Yes sir!
SQUIRE LI.
> On love in the bower I riveted my eyes,
> never thought the real winner'd ever claim his prize!

LUO *and* MRS LUO. Well, it would be a cheek to show our faces here
any longer, so the best thing we can do is pretend we're going
with Squire Li to the county court and slip off unnoticed.

81

Let's do like the turtle when it gets a fright:
heads in our shells and the world's out of sight!

(*Exeunt attendants, Squire Li, Luo and Mrs Luo.*)

OLD MRS QIU. Now, daughter-in-law, if you won't be reconciled to
my son, I shall put an end to my life.
PLUM-BLOSSOM BEAUTY. (*Sings*)
Oh, you put me in such a dread,
like a fawn trots my heart, oh the fright!
Let's discuss things, and then I'm sure
everything will be all right.
(*Says*) Dear mother-in-law, I'll have Qiu Hu back again after all.
OLD MRS QIU. If you'll have Qiu Hu back, then I shan't commit
suicide.
PLUM-BLOSSOM BEAUTY. Fine, just fine! (*Sings*)
That's the trouble with us women, no stamina or stay,
too *mobile*!
OLD MRS QIU. Since you've agreed to have Qiu Hu back, you can go
and change your dress and make yourself look pretty, and then
you and he can formally make it up by paying your courteous
respects to one another.

(*Plum-Blossom Beauty goes off, comes back dressed and made up more like a
lady, and bows with Qiu Hu to Old Mrs Qiu. Then Plum-Blossom Beauty and
Qiu Hu bow to one another.*)

PLUM-BLOSSOM BEAUTY. (*Sings*)
But for our dear old mother who needs our loving care,
our marriage would have broken beyond hope of repair.
Today I cast aside rough hairpins hewn of wood
to don the garb and finery a noble lady should.
Yes, now together we'll both share
your glory that will long endure.
I was not being awkward just for fun,
not affecting moods or seeking false quarrels:
I just felt obliged to vindicate
the constancy of my wifely morals;
Luofu escaped more easily in that tale of ancient days,
all she had to do for a moment or two
was lie to her wooer, sing her husband's praise!
QIU HU. Of all the happy things in the world, there is none that
surpasses the joy of a mother and child reunited and a husband
and wife brought together again. So now we must slaughter a

82

sheep and prepare some wine and hold a party to celebrate all our good fortune.

Let us recall how, married joys scarce started,
I was enlisted, and suddenly we parted.
Since in grief I quit my mother and wife,
the planets have trekked the sky
and the world turned its changes ten years of our life.
But fortune blessed me with success,
brocade robes replaced battledress.
My lord gave me gold for my mother's care,
to keep her provided with dainty fare.
Then I met in the mulberry-grove my wife of humbler days,
and sought to force her love, as if driven by some foolish
    craze:
but, virtue irreducible, she proved quite unseducible,
and guarded so well her chastity as to merit a niche in history.
And to this present day when strangers pass this way
and make their due inquiries about the local life,
there are elders old and grey who will know the tale and say:
'Here Qiu Hu once attempted to seduce his wedded wife.'

End Titles:[1]

    Virtuous Plum-Blossom Beauty guards her chastity with her
      life,
    The Honorable Qiu Hu, minister of Lu, tries to seduce his
      own wife.

'Secret liaison with Chancellor Bo Pi'

Act VII from *chuanqi* play *Washing silk* by Liang Chenyu
(1520–*c*.1580)

Characters:
CHANCELLOR BO PI: chancellor of the kingdom of Wu.
BATMAN: of Bo Pi.
MYRIAD CHARMS: chubby concubine of Bo Pi.
WEN ZHONG: minister of Yue.
RETINUE: of Wen Zhong.
GUARD: in the camp of Bo Pi.
SERVANT: of Bo Pi.
AUTUMN SWAN and SPRING SWALLOW: beautiful maidens.

(*Enter Chancellor Bo Pi.*)

CHANCELLOR BO PI. (*Sings*)
    Serried camps and armies brigaded,
    our great banners to the fore,
    Vermilion Bird flags[1] directing us south.
    Armour stands arrayed
    mid bows and swords in bristling cluster,
    as ten thousand mounted men 'south of the city walls'[2]
    return victorious from battle.
    Tell me now:
    what heroes has this land to match us?
    (*Says*)
    And who can rival me,
    my might, my frame, my awesome looks? –
    though I never mastered weaponry,
    nor got the hang of civil books.
    When my men march in, then I opt out,
    it's up to them how the battles go,
    for these two mighty hands of mine
    have never slain a single foe.
Chancellor Bo Pi, that's me. By nature surpassing the mother-eating vulture and the father-eating muntjak-leopard [a mythical bird and a mythical beast]. More ferocious than tiger or wolf. The bladed cunning I conceal within me is of a thousand forms and

ten thousand mutations, beyond the ken of devil or demon, and when I lay my plots and set my traps, disaster strikes from a million paths and none can ward against it. Well apprenticed in the deployment of cunning stratagems, master in the subtle sowing of doubt and consternation. Sword-tongued I am, and spear-lipped, slave-woman-faced and serving-girl-kneed. When I bow, you would think my body had no bones. My joking is like hidden knives. All my endeavour resides in fawning flattery and complaisance to one man. Kindness to the common mass is beyond my scope and savvy. And this has sent me soaring, hoisted me high among the nations of the world, and given me power second to none in all the royal court. When the fox goes walking in tag with the tiger, he has no fear of falling prey to other beasts. When the little rat settles down by the state altar, he no longer dreads they'll smoke and burn him out. By being ever bitterly jealous of men of ability and virtue, you can secure your position, and draw your salary with no more effort than a corpse.

These last couple of days I have been in command of our advance army, chasing the men of Yue, the brigand scum. In one long forced march, we have penetrated deep into Yue, and are laying siege to their capital, Kuaiji. So here I am, perched on this mountain. My mighty army is not yet preparing to return to Wu, but we're worn out and weary from the constant fighting and haven't been able to snatch the slightest respite. There is a lull in military activity this evening, so I'll just relieve myself of my armour and helmet for a while. Must send my batman with orders to my subordinate officers to keep a tight guard on the gates of our fortified encampment, and to report to me immediately should there be any military developments. Hey you, you rascal, where are you!

(*Enter batman. He conveys the orders in a loud voice, and there is a backstage response of 'orders received!'*)

CHANCELLOR BO PI. Since the old days when I first fled to Wu from my homeland, Chu, I've never taken a wife. There's a real hardship, and no mistake! But the other day I got hold of a wench called Myriad Charms. Not exactly the height of delicate refinement and grace to look at, but she's got a way of making herself up to look quite seductive. What I like about her is the way she can massage you. Marvellous. And she knows a thing or two in bed, too. Just that her manners are a bit coarse. Bit of a jealous nagging tyrant as well. The other day, because we were short of staff here in the army, I brought her up here to attend to my needs, but the last couple of days I've had no leisure for her. Been

terribly neglecting her, so I must call her here, and have a little
tête-à-tête, a spot of passion. Yes, that's a good idea! Where are
you, Myriad Charms?

(*Enter fat woman.*)

MYRIAD CHARMS. (*Sings*)
　　If it's romance you're after in life,
　　well, you won't do better than the Chancellor's wife!
　　Her dear tiny feet, fifteen inches long,
　　patter along like billy-oh,
　　her delicate eyebrows, ten inches each,
　　are curved like a double-bent bow.
　　All say she's a light and airy baby,
　　but feel perhaps that she is maybe
　　a teeny-weeny dose too gross.
(*Says*) Your Excellency, I kowtow before you.

CHANCELLOR BO PI. Rise to your feet, dear Myriad Charms! Myriad
Charms, I've been so busy with this war the last couple of days that
I haven't managed to see you. I've been longing for you no end.

MYRIAD CHARMS. And me for you, too, Your Excellency. I've been
yearning for you so much these last few days that I've quite been
off my food, only eating half as much as usual.

CHANCELLOR BO PI. What did you have for breakfast, then?

MYRIAD CHARMS. Well, I was feeling a tiny bit more cheerful this
morning, so I got through eight bowlfuls.

CHANCELLOR BO PI. And what about lunch?

MYRIAD CHARMS. I felt a bit down in the dumps at midday, so I
couldn't eat much. I had to force myself just to eat five bowlfuls.

CHANCELLOR BO PI. Eh, that sounds a fair amount to me!

MYRIAD CHARMS. Oh, usually, when I'm feeling well, I can eat a
few more bowlfuls than that! Now because I've cut down on my
food, my waist looks as if I'm wasting away.

CHANCELLOR BO PI. Ah yes, as the old saying goes: 'The King of
Chu loved dainty waists, so the palace ladies all starved to death'!

MYRIAD CHARMS. Stop making fun of me!

CHANCELLOR BO PI. I'm really worn and weary this last day or so.
Give me a massage.

(*She gives him a massage.*)

CHANCELLOR BO PI. Myriad Charms, my heart's delight, when you
press my cavity-sinuses³ and pinch my ticklish spots, my skin
tingles, my bones feel light and airy, and I feel soothed and
smooth and helpless all over, and can't move a muscle. Ooh, it's
lovely!

MYRIAD CHARMS. My lord, that's nothing. Stop a mo', jump on the bed, fix this needle, and nail this cavity, and it'll be lovelier still!

CHANCELLOR BO PI. Myriad Charms, there's someone coming outside my command tent. You'd better make yourself scarce for a jiffy.

MYRIAD CHARMS. Hurry up and send them away, then make haste and join me in bed.

(*Exit Myriad Charms. Enter Wen Zhong leading his retinue, to deliver his presents of gold.*)

WEN ZHONG. (*Sings*)
> Clandestinely I bear my gifts of gold,
> having ascertained that the vanguard of their army
> lies just west of the River Zhe.

(*Says*) Travelling during the daytime is fraught with difficulties, so, waiting till dusk and darkness, I have disguised myself as an officer of the Wu army, and am now proceeding upon my mission. (*Sings*)
> Travelling in the day
> would draw, I fear, too many suspicions,
> So, awaiting twilight when stars come sparse,
> I suddenly take my stealthy departure,
> unseen by any watching eyes.

(*Says*) Is there anyone here before the tent of command to announce me?

GUARD. What is your name, Captain? What urgent business brings you here in the dark of night?

WEN ZHONG. I am Wen Zhong, a minister of the State of Yue. I want to see your commander. May I trouble you to announce us to him?

GUARD. We're in a state of military alert. I can't comply with your request. Wouldn't dare.

WEN ZHONG. Might I offer you these hundred taels of silver, as some small token of my gratitude? Just say that I have something to ask of him himself, which is why I come in the dark of night.

GUARD. Ah, now in that case, just wait here a while. (*Enters and announces*) Wen Zhong, envoy from the State of Yue, wishes to seek a favour, and comes here in the dark of night for that purpose.

CHANCELLOR BO PI. Hm, odd, very odd! What's he come for? Never mind, show him in.

WEN ZHONG. Wen Zhong, worthless minister from the Kingdom of Yue, comes to pay his respects.

CHANCELLOR BO PI. (*In a fury*) So you are Wen Zhong!

WEN ZHONG. Dare I say yes?

CHANCELLOR BO PI. You're the one who before we joined battle the other day hailed me as a shameless rogue!

WEN ZHONG. Dare I say yes?

CHANCELLOR BO PI. You hurled abuse at me, said I was a faithless minister and a wicked heartless son, a treacherous, toadying courtier.

WEN ZHONG. Dare I say yes?

CHANCELLOR BO PI. With the imminent approach of my monarch's royal forces, you are on the eve of destruction. What's the point of your visiting me?

WEN ZHONG. Your Excellency, my dear Chancellor, please calm your anger, and permit me to present my supplication to you.

CHANCELLOR BO PI. What is there to be said? Out with it, then!

WEN ZHONG. Goujian, meagre monarch of our insignificant kingdom, is filled with gratitude for all your kindnesses, Chancellor, and although lacking the means adequately to repay you –

CHANCELLOR BO PI. (*Anger suddenly changing to smiles*) Oho, so that good old fellow, your King of Yue, realizes how grateful he should be to me, too, does he?

WEN ZHONG. Indeed, he does, and has specially sent me with a few presents for you, mere token gifts.

CHANCELLOR BO PI. (*Guffawing with sheer delight*) Oh, you really shouldn't have put yourself out so much. Coming all this way! Too generous of you! Rise, I beg you.

WEN ZHONG. Too kind. The presents are all outside your command tent. As I have brought a lot of people with me, I shall have them each proffer you one present in turn, one at a time, and only upon your deigning to call out your acceptance will they venture to present them to you. Now here come these gifts: five thousand ounces of yellow gold, five thousand bolts of brocade silk, and ten pairs of white jade orbs.

CHANCELLOR BO PI. How can I accept so much? You, knave, servant, slaughter a sheep, heat up some wine, and show my lord Wen to a seat.

(*Servant assents, exit*)

WEN ZHONG. My dear Chancellor, I bid you stay your delight a while: I still have a couple of things, live things, but I'm rather apprehensive of offering them to you, for fear you may consider them utterly useless.

CHANCELLOR BO PI. What are they? Bring 'em on, and let's have a look at 'em.

WEN ZHONG. Let me go and fetch them.

(*Enter Autumn Swan and Spring Swallow.*)

AUTUMN SWAN *and* SPRING SWALLOW. (*Say*)
The moon above the weeping-willow bower
sinks from its dancing,
the breeze beneath the fan of peach blossoms
ceases its singing.

WEN ZHONG. My poor monarch, King Goujian, lacking sufficient means to convey his respect, and having heard that Your Excellency the Chancellor has not yet married, for these reasons humbly offers you these two beautiful women, the one being called Autumn Swan, and the other Spring Swallow, so that they may provide you with some company upon your pillow and between your sheets. I beg you to favour them with your gaze, and pray that you will think fit to accept them.

AUTUMN SWAN and SPRING SWALLOW. We kowtow before you, Your Excellency.

CHANCELLOR BO PI. (*Giggling*) Rise to your feet, dear beautiful ladies, I implore you. Servant! Slaughter an ox.

(*Comic actions, as before. Responses from backstage.*)

CHANCELLOR BO PI. My dear Minister Wen, my dear Lord Wen, what understanding you have for the trend of my little foibles! To be quite frank and open with you, it is true that I have never had a missus all these years, but recently I hired a little bird, just to keep me going. She's quite a graceful, sexy piece, but nowhere near as attractive as these two charming ladies. I'll take them both in turn, this one tonight and that one tomorrow night, and so on, one come, one go, one up, one down. Lovely, lovely fun! – Ah, but hang on a moment: your sovereign Lord has given me all these presents. I wonder how I might oblige him in return? What were his instructions?

WEN ZHONG. My monarch told me to convey his deepest regards to you, Chancellor. He is deeply grateful for all the advice and enlightment he has received from your great King of Wu and you yourself, Your Excellency, and is now only too glad to lead his wives and his ministers to Wu, that he himself may there become the King of Wu's subject and his wives may become the King of Wu's concubines, if your sovereign so graciously permits. But, fearing that the King of Wu might be indisposed to consent to this, he has sent me on ahead to convey his respects to yourself, Chancellor. We hope and beg for succour and protection.

CHANCELLOR BO PI. In view of all these favours I have just had from your king, I am completely at his service. I can do the trifling things he asks of me without the slightest difficulty. Hey, servant!

(*Enter servant.*)

CHANCELLOR BO PI. I told you to slaughter a sheep and an ox. Where are they all this time? Why haven't you produced them?
SERVANT. Beg leave to inform Your Excellency, there don't happen to be any sheep or oxen. Only one chicken. And Lady Myriad Charms won't let us have that, either!
CHANCELLOR BO PI. Ridiculous! Why won't she?
SERVANT. She's heard that two pretty women have just been brought in as presents for you. Perhaps she's a bit jealous.
CHANCELLOR BO PI. Tcha! We seem to have been caught off guard for the moment, with inadequate provisions for your entertainment. Just bring a bit of wine and some snacks. Must apologize most profusely for all this flurry and lack of proper courtesy, my good Lord Wen.
WEN ZHONG. Not at all! Not at all!
CHANCELLOR BO PI. (*Sings*)
> I thank your monarch for keeping me in mind,
> for the gold and the silk and regards most kind,
> for the jewel-sets, the heaps of gems and pearls,
> for the pair of blossom-buds, these comely dainty girls,
> I'm a man of honour true,
> and when gratitude is due
> the stork of luck will wing your way;
> don't underrate Bo Pi's friendship,
> he'll do a good turn or two.
> Hurry up to our land of Wu,
> do not dally or delay,
> and I guarantee that from its cage
> the stork of luck will wing your way.

WEN ZHONG. My monarch (*Sings*)
> Despatched this embassy here,
> being mindful how brokenly he lingers in Kuaiji,
> and desirous in person to lead his wives and slaves
> into the court of Wu,
> there gladly, with all due ceremony, to render his homage as
>   vassal.
> Tomorrow I shall see my king once more:
> I pray you may contrive to afford us your protection.

CHANCELLOR BO PI. Leave it all to me. No need to din it in!
WEN ZHONG. (*Sings*)
> Deep is my gratitude for your lofty clemency, my lord.
> Should we be spared harsh treatment and abuse,

I swear to be your dog, your horse,
in my scurrying haste to serve you.
(*Says*) Autumn Swan, Spring Swallow, serve us some wine.
AUTUMN SWAN and SPRING SWALLOW. (*Sing*)
Cloudy tresses and towered curls,
swirling skirts come dancing, sewn with birds of love.
When spring breezes waft,
laugh and hug amid the flowers;
when autumn evenings fall,
slumber drunk on boudoir couches.
Sip love, quaff love,
for how many in this life attain a hundred years?
Tonight let's ecstasy together,
dream-souls flying,
two sunset clouds a-homing to the Pinnacle of Love.
WEN ZHONG. Take good care of His Excellency, both of you, and
serve him with the utmost diligence. I shall now take my leave of
you, your Excellency, and shall meet you again tomorrow to the
fore of our army.
CHANCELLOR BO PI. My good Lord Wen, there is just another very
important thing I must tell you first. The Prime Minister of my
country, Wu Zixu, is an awkward, pig-headed character, no tact
or give-and-take whatsoever. If he turns up on the scene
tomorrow, he's bound to be a stumbling-block. I'm in command
of the advance forces besieging this side of Mount Kuaiji, and he's
in command of the rear forces surrounding the other side of the
mountain. We are due to meet the King as usual around noon. So
you, Minister Wen, must join me very early in the morning, and
we'll set off together, so that, before Wu Zixu arrives, we shall
have had the chance for me to intervene and settle things and gain
the King of Wu's own verbal agreement to our arrangements.
Once we've done that, even if Wu Zixu turns up he'll be too late to
do anything about it!
WEN ZHONG. I shall do exactly as you command. (*Exit*)
CHANCELLOR BO PI. Autumn Swan, Spring Swallow ... isn't it
marvellous, two tender charmers like yourselves meeting up with
such a dashing lady-killer as myself! It's just like they say: a
wedding fixed by ancient destiny, 'twixt brilliant man and
peerless beauty. We musn't split up tonight: the three of us can
share one bed, eh?

(*Makes to go off, with an arm round each of the girls. Enter Myriad Charms.
She starts lashing out at Autumn Swan and Spring Swallow.*)

MYRIAD CHARMS. Very nice, very nice! What sort of rotten sluts are you? Where do you come from, you hussies? Coming here and grabbing my business from me! Clear out! At once! Clear out! CHANCELLOR BO PI. (*Clouting Myriad Charms*) You stinking whore! You perishing trollop! You brazen bitch! You thick-skinned baggage! Get back to your room! Get back to your room!

(*Exeunt.*)

Wolf of Mount Zhong

Brief *zaju* play by Wang Jiusi (1468–1551)

Characters:

KING JIANZI OF ZHAO: King of the Warring States kingdom of Zhao.
GUARDS: of King Jianzi.
MASTER DONGGUO: philosopher of the philosophical school of Mo Di.
WOLF OF MOUNT ZHONG.
SOLDIER: one of King Jianzi's men.
OLD APRICOT-TREE.
OLD OX.
OLD LOCAL DEITY: the Earth God of Mount Zhong, disguised as an old man.
LITTLE DEMON: in the service of the Local Deity.

(Enter the King of Zhao at the head of his guards, who are carrying bows and arrows and other hunting implements.)

KING. I am King Jianzi of Zhao. I have come out with some of my soldiers this morning to do some hunting among these hills. We encountered a savage wolf, and I shot at it but missed. Now it has made off ahead of us. Come, my officers and men, hasten forward in pursuit!

(Enter Master Dongguo, with a donkey which bears his book-trunk on its back.)

DONGGUO. I am Master Dongguo, and I'm from the land of Yan. All my life I have followed the doctrines of Mo Di[1], which have as their basic theme that one should try to succour mankind and do good to all creatures on earth. The other day a letter came from the King of Wei inviting me to go to his kingdom to expound these doctrines, and I felt compelled to set off for Wei. I have been travelling for the last few days, and now suddenly find myself in the region of Mount Zhong, here in the Kingdom of Zhao. On we go now. Ah, what's that I can see in the distance – a crowd of people on horseback coming this way. *(Peers into the distance.)* Ah, now I can see: why, it's a band of mounted huntsmen. Such a wild and tumultuous hunt I've never seen in all my life! *(Sings)*
   With the early morning breezes and last of the fading moon,
   I come to Mount Zhong.

What on earth is happening?
All these galloping horses and scurrying men!
A smoke of dust for scores of miles!
Such a variety of weapons!
Ah, now I see, it's officers hunting;
I have never seen such an impetuous onrush.

(*The King of Zhao and his men catch up with Master Dongguo. A soldier comes over to question Dongguo.*)

SOLDiER. You, standing by the roadside, who are you?

DONGGUO. I'm Master Dongguo from the country of Yan. I am on my way to the Kingdom of Wei, and am just passing through this land.

SOLDIER. A minute ago a wolf escaped us and it must have come this way. You're bound to have seen it. Speak up, quickly! – Which way did it go?

DONGGUO. No, I haven't seen it. I certainly haven't seen it.

SOLDIER. What have you got in that trunk? I think I'll search it.

DONGGUO. It's got books inside. (*Sings*)

My luggage is very simple and sparse,
my trunk is fairly packed with books,
the classics of poetry and history.

SOLDIER. Why aren't you on the move? What are you doing just waiting around here?

DONGGUO. (*Sings*)

My lame donkey ambles very slow,
my road is long, the going's hard on foot.

SOLDIER. (*Searches the trunk, then says*) If you've seen the wolf, you'd better speak up, and look quick about it! Don't try and trick me!

DONGGUO. (*Sings*)

If I had seen it, would I dare to lie?
The wolf must have found a path
of refuge from calamity.

SOLDIER. If you've been swindling me, I'll kill you! (*Draws sword, and hacks at the ground with it.*)

DONGGUO. (*Sings*)

Do not be so vicious.
What cause could you have to kill
a solitary wayfaring fellow like me?

KING. If he has not seen the wolf, let him be! Let us pursue our hunt with all haste. (*Exit King.*)

DONGGUO. Just my ill-luck! For no reason at all, I have to bump into such villainous knaves! They were nearly the end of me – I'd better pause here, and recover for a while.

(Huntsmen and soldiers make off in pursuit of the wolf once more. Exeunt. Enter wolf.)

WOLF. I am the Wolf of Mount Zhong. This morning the King of Zhao has come out hunting, and he shot an arrow at me. He missed, but now they're hot on my tracks! What on earth can I do? *(Points towards Dongguo)* There's someone sitting down over there in the distance. I'll go and seek his help. *(Presents himself before Dongguo)* Master! Master! Save my life!

DONGGUO. Why, you must be that wolf those horsemen were chasing. Aren't you?

WOLF. Yes, yes, the very one. I hope above hope that you will save my life, master.

DONGGUO. *Me* save *your* life! Just now I almost lost my own life because of you. I'm just a traveller on my way through; how can I rescue you?

WOLF. Master, if you took all the books out of that trunk of yours, and hid me in it, that would save me without a doubt!

DONGGUO. But you're quite a size, and the trunk is only small. I couldn't fit you inside it.

WOLF. There's one way it can be done. See, on the donkey's saddle: there's a rope kept there for emergencies. Fetch it here, and rope my paws together, tie my head down onto my breast, and stuff me into the trunk. After you've done that, lock up the trunk and put it on the donkey's back. Then not even someone with a 'thousand-mile eye', let alone the King of Zhao and his horsemen, would know that I was inside it.

DONGGUO. All right, then, all right! I'll do as you say. And if you survive, be grateful to me!

WOLF. How could I ever think to forget your generous kindness, master? I'll repay you for it some day, if needs be with my own life!

(Dongguo ropes up the wolf and puts him in the trunk, and with the trunk on the donkey's back, they make off.)

WOLF. *(Jumping round inside the box, shouts)* Master, how far away do you think the huntsmen are?

DONGGUO. I can still see them.

WOLF. If that's the case, hurry the donkey up a bit!

DONGGUO. All right, then, all right.

(They flee onward for a little while more.)

WOLF. Master, do you think we're far enough away from them now? I'm being strangled to death by these ropes in here.

DONGGUO. We're a good long way away from them now. I can't see them any more.

WOLF. If that's so, will you take me out of here, then?

(*Dungguo unlocks the trunk, takes the wolf out, and undoes the ropes.*)

DONGGUO. Oh wolf, oh wolf! You've escaped with your life.

WOLF. And you with yours, master ...! (*Bows his thanks*) When shall I ever be able to repay this great kindness you have done me? Should I ever prove ungrateful to you, master, it will be no more than I deserve if the judgements of Heaven and Earth sentence me to gradual dismemberment and death by ten thousand cuts of the knife.

DONGGUO. All my life I have made it my fundamental principle to succour others and benefit all things in creation. So how should I expect you to repay any kindness that I may have done you? Off you go now, free to wander as you will.

(*Wolf takes his leave of Dongguo, and makes off. Then he ponders.*)

WOLF. I've been hunted by the King of Zhao and his horsemen since this morning, harassed the whole day long. Now it's getting late, and I'm starving hungry, and I won't be able to find any small animals to eat anywhere. That philosopher has just saved my life, but if I'm going to starve to death now anyway, what was the use of being saved? That philosopher seemed to be a compassionate man ... Yes, that's it! That's what I must do. I'll go and see if I can find him, and discuss the matter with him.

(*Wolf catches up with Dongguo, and they greet each other.*)

DONGGUO. What are you doing here again?

WOLF. A little something I'd like to discuss with you, master.

DONGGUO. What is it? Out with it!

WOLF. I've gone without anything to eat all day since this morning, and my stomach is empty, so I've come to ask for your help, master.

DONGGUO. So you've come to ask me for help? But how do you expect me to be able to find you anything? I'm hungry, too, and I haven't even got anything to eat for myself.

WOLF. I've got a marvellous idea, but it's rather a delicate matter, and I feel too embarrassed to tell you.

DONGGUO. A marvellous idea, eh? Well, what is it? Don't be afraid, just go ahead and tell me about it, then we can both discuss how to carry it out.

WOLF. Yes, yes, it is a marvellous idea, but all the same it's rather awkward to explain. You try and guess it, master.

DONGGUO. It doesn't come to me for the moment. Hurry up, tell me what it is.

WOLF. Master, master, you've saved me once. But if I'm to starve to death now, it would have been better if you hadn't saved me.

DONGGUO. In that case, what do you plan to do about it?

WOLF. (*Looking embarrassed and perplexed once more, kowtows, and says*) Master, it would be best if you were to let me eat you, and then I can repay both your kindnesses together some day.

(*Wolf makes to bite Dongguo.*)

DONGGUO. Heavens above! This creature has no morals whatsoever! I saved his life, and now he wants to eat me! What on earth do you mean by such base ingratitude?

WOLF. Master! Just look at the human beings in this world! Each togged up in coat and hat, looking all civilized, and every man jack of them claiming to be a good fellow and a gentleman of true virtue. But if others chance to treat them with any generous kindness or love, they just forget all about it. And if they meet with any opportunity to take unfair advantage of others, they grasp it without ado. And then there are all those treacherous ministers and disloyal sons[2] – what sins are they incapable of committing? *I'm* nothing but an animal, so how can you blame *me* for ingratitude? How am I any worse than human beings?

DONGGUO. Such glib and specious words are all uttered solely so that you may eat me. I won't allow myself to waste any anger on you. People in ancient times used to have the saying:

If you've a matter you cannot decide,
in three old men your problem confide.

So let us both walk on for a bit, and if we meet anyone we'll ask him whether you should eat me or not.

WOLF. All right then, all right then. We'll do as you say, master.

(*Enter old apricot-tree. It stands still.*)

DONGGUO. (*Pointing towards the apricot-tree*) That seems to be someone standing over there in the distance. We can go over together, and put our question to him ... Ah, here we are, we've reached him. But why! It's an old apricot-tree! Can't be helped, we must ask him all the same ... Old apricot-tree, listen a moment, will you. This wolf was hunted by the King of Zhao's men, and was pursued until he was at his wits' end with fear. He begged me to rescue him, so I hid him in my book-trunk, and saved his life. And now he wants to eat me! Tell me, old apricot-tree: should he do so, or not?

APRICOT-TREE. Yes, he should eat you.

DONGGUO. Why should he eat me?

APRICOT-TREE. Three or four years after my master planted me I bore apricots. All the family, grown-ups and children alike, ate them. Guests were served with them, and people were given them as presents. So who knows how many must have been eaten over the years! Now I'm forty years of age, and, seeing that I don't bear apricots any more, they have chopped off my branches for firewood. And soon they'll come and chop down this solitary trunk of mine. I have shown them generosity and love these forty or fifty years, and yet they are still utterly ungrateful. You only rescued him on the spur of the moment – what ground is that for gratitude? Yes, he *should* eat you! He *should* eat you!

(*Wolf makes to bite Dongguo. Dongguo dodges out of the way.*)

DONGGUO. (*Sings*)
>Walking along in this wild open land,
>we found an old apricot-tree to whom we put our case.
>His verdict was
>the wolf should make a meal of me.
>How can I talk my way out of this plight?

>   Ah me, 'tis ever the same:
>when ground has been flat,
>bumps appear from nowhere.
>Truly I stand helpless in this vile dilemma.
>This aconite³ vermin
>not only fails to repay my kindness,
>but now the poison-hearted wolf
>would pierce me through the breast!
>Bitter pangs invade my soul!
>Yes, true it is, as I now see,
>that 'wolves hate goodness in mens' hearts'.
>Where can I turn to plead my cause?
>Yes, to be sure,
>'Heaven is high and the Emperor far!'

Now that we've met this old apricot-tree and he says I ought to be eaten, what on earth can I do? Wolf! You agreed beforehand that we should ask *three* people, and we've only asked one up to now. Let us proceed further.

(*Enter an old ox. Comes to a standstill.*)

DONGGUO. (*Pointing towards the ox*) I wonder who that is standing over there ahead of us? Let's both go and put our problem to him. Ah, here we are in front of him ... Why, it's an old ox. (*Goes up to ox, and puts his question)* This wolf was being hunted by the King of Zhao and his horsemen until he was at the end of his tether. He came to me for help, and I saved his life by hiding him in my book-trunk. Tell me in fairness and truth: should he eat me, or should he not eat me?

OX. He should eat you!

DONGGUO. *(Angrily)* What do you mean, he should eat me?

OX. Just you listen to me. This master of mine reared me from a calf, and later when I grew bigger I ploughed the fields for him, rolled the grain to husk it for him, and dragged his carts for him, until all my sinews were overstrained, and my strength exhausted. Now, noticing that I've grown old and can't do anything strenuous, he has just abandoned me out here in the wilds. 'If this ox has lost its strength,' said my master, 'then let *us* lose *it*.' As if that wasn't bad enough, his wife went one worse, the long-tongued, vicious woman. 'What's the good of keeping on feeding this ox?' she said. 'Let's waste no time, and find a butcher to slaughter it. Then we can sell its hide to the musicians for stretching over their drums. We can sell its meat to the butcher. Its horns we can sell to the hairpin-makers, and the bones we'll keep to heat up and make paint for use in the house. Don't you think that's a wonderful idea?' So it won't be more than a couple of days before they'll be coming to put an end to me. All the many great kindnesses I did to that family have been forgotten. So where does all your gratitude stuff come into it? He *should* eat you! Yes, he *should* eat you!

(Wolf makes to bite Dongguo. Dongguo dodges out of the way.)

DONGGUO. *(Sings)*
It's all your fault, old ox,
you and your treachery!
He sharpens his teeth,
his eyes glare wide,
I'm truly due to be his meal.
No point in procrastinating,
let him destroy me here and now!
Oh, Heaven!
Foul plight,
such anguish on my brow,
and in these tear-filled eyes.
By trying to escape
I only deepen my danger.

WOLF. Both of them have said I should eat you, master. Hurry up and let me devour you, will you? I'm starving to death.

DONGGUO. Since we agreed to it, we must just ask one more person, and then I shall gladly allow you to eat me.

(*They walk on together again. Enter an old man leaning on a walking-staff.*)

LOCAL DEITY. I am the God of the Soil of Mount Zhong, the local deity. Just now one of my little demons came and reported to me that there was a travelling scholar here who had saved a wolf's life, and that the wolf was now actually trying to eat him. What sort of behaviour is that? So I have changed myself into an old man, and I'm going to deal with the matter!

(*Old man continues walking.*)

DONGGUO. (*Pointing at the old man*) Look over there, there's an elderly gentleman approaching. Let's go over and question him, to see what he says about it. (*Presents himself before the old man, and kneels down.*) Venerable sir, this wolf was being hunted by the King of Zhao, and was pursued so hotly that in his frantic terror he begged me to rescue him. I hid him in my book-trunk, and saved his life, but then he said that he wanted to eat me. I told him the saying:
>   If you've a matter you cannot decide,
>   your problem in three old men confide.

We've already put the question to an old apricot-tree, and the apricot-tree said that it was right for him to eat me. And we've asked an old ox, who also said he should eat me. Now, by good fortune, we have encountered you, venerable sir, and I hope you will deliver me from this injustice.

LOCAL DEITY. Call the wolf over here! ... Is it or is it not a fact that this scholar rescued you?

WOLF. Yes, he rescued me all right, but not out of any goodness of his heart.

LOCAL DEITY. What do you mean, not out of any goodness of his heart?

WOLF. Well, when he did it, he tied me up with a rope and put me in his book-trunk, intending to do away with me. But luckily I've got a charmed life, and I came out of it alive. And now I want to eat him, just for my due revenge. I pray that you will grant us the discretion of your judgement, venerable sir.

LOCAL DEITY. (*Calling Dongguo over to him*) What on earth got into you, saving a wretch like that? Just a moment, and I'll deal with the matter for you. (*Calls wolf*) Wolf! In spite of what you said, I really cannot bring myself to believe it – you're so big, and the book-trunk is so small. How could it hold you? Tell me the truth, now! And if we discover that he did indeed intend to kill you, you must obtain your revenge here and now, and he must be eaten up by you in just requittal.

WOLF. He did put me inside the book-trunk, honestly he did! I would never dare lie to you.

LOCAL DEITY. Nonetheless, I cannot find it in me to believe you until I have actually seen you put inside the trunk once more. Then the scholar, too, will have to resign himself to the truth and allow you to eat him without grudge or protest.

WOLF. Very well, then, very well!

LOCAL DEITY. (*Calls Dongguo over*) Tie him up, and put him in the book-trunk, exactly as you did before, just to show me.

(*Dongguo ties up the wolf, puts him in the trunk, and locks it.*)

LOCAL DEITY. So it really was true, after all! That scoundrel of a wolf is completely lacking in morality. Kill him at once, now! Kill him at once! Isn't that a sword you have at your waist, scholar?

DONGGUO. Yes, it is.

LOCAL DEITY. Since you have this sword, why didn't you kill him with it before? Instead of letting him put you in such straits!

DONGGUO. I am a student and follower of that doctrine which urges one to succour others and love all creatures, so how could I bear to kill him?

LOCAL DEITY. (*Laughs*) You are on the wrong track, scholar! You would do better to follow Confucius's and Mencius's doctrines of kindliness allied to moral rightness[4]. Why must you adhere to those principles of doting, indiscriminate love? Haven't you heard that 'If you don't strike while the iron's hot, you only forge your own ruination'? That's just how it is with such a fellow as you, with your muddled head always up in the clouds!

DONGGUO. Yes, thanks to your advice, venerable sir, I realize now that I was wrong. But I couldn't bring myself to kill him.

WOLF. (*Calling out from inside the trunk*) Stop playing around! Hurry up and let me out of here, so I can eat him in revenge.

(*Enter little demon.*)

LITTLE DEMON. Scholar! Will you still not kill him? (*Snatches the sword, and sets about killing the wolf. The wolf yells out.*)

DONGGUO. Listen, wolf, (*Sings*)
> You tricked me before,
> used me to save your own skin,
> and when you were safe and sound
> you forgot all the peril you'd undergone.
> In base ingratitude

you conceived a cunning notion
and nearly made a 'feast of this philosopher'[5].

  Ah, my love was broad as the ocean wide,
but, your conscience dead,
you gave greed its head,
and your crime was as big as a mountain.
But if *you* were so wicked and cunning,
I was shown up as dull and dumb-dogged:
failing to recognize evil,
failing to recognize treachery's face.
To think how I met you on the road,
and just blundered into the Gates of Death.
Again and again you tried to murder me,
yet still you bluster against your fate!

  Ah me, yes, truly:
'kindness is easy enough to distribute,
but it's hard to find debts of gratitude paid!'
Easy to err, but hard to go back on one's error.
And, don't you think, human beings are sly,
treacherous and cunning,
for all their human-looking faces,
And their hearts are the image of this wild wolf's.

End titles:

  King Jianzi of Zhao holds a mighty hunt,
Dongguo harms himself by his own behaviour,
The Local Deity rights a wrong,
and the Wolf of Mount Zhong tries to kill his own saviour.

Buying rouge

Early Qing farce: anon., eighteenth century

Characters:

WANG MOON BLOOM: pretty young daughter of a woman who keeps a cosmetics shop; serves in the shop.

GUO HUA: young scholar gentleman.

ITINERANT SALESMAN: a pedlar or haberdasher.

(*Enter Wang Moon Bloom.*)

MOON BLOOM. (*Sings*)
> Since I met that student lad,
> the thought of him has kept me glad,
> and if some day I can marry that man,
> make him mine for ever more,
> it will put my heart for ever at ease,
> sweetly serene and secure.

(*Says*) When I set eyes on that fine young blade,
> I was smitten through and through,
> I yearn to meet him again – but we made,
> alas, no rendezvous.
> All day long in languid despair,
> I lack the appetite to drink or eat,
> I'm too love-listless to tidy my raven hair,
> to make my blue-black tresses neat.

I'm Wang Moon Bloom. Our family has always lived here outside Changan city and kept a rouge and cosmetics shop. It was very sad, my father passed away the year before last, so me and my mother, just the two of us, were left to try and keep house and home together. It's a hard struggle, but luckily my mother is still in good health and has a knack for managing things. Anyway, that's not what I'm supposed to be talking about. The other day a young scholar gentleman kept on coming into our shop to purchase rouge, and exchanging lovey-dovey glances with me, and chatting me up really passionately. But what could I do? There was my mother standing next to me, so I couldn't get on chatting terms with him. And so it made me feel even more gloomy than I was to start with. Today my mother's gone round to some relative's. Maybe that young gentleman will come and buy some rouge from us again. You can never tell. I'll just open the shop door, and see what luck may drop my way out of the blue.

(*Sings*)

Open the shop door nice and wide,
then hang our shop sign up outside:
'Our rouge and cosmetics everywhere we sell,
in the southern capital and the northern one as well.
We proffer our excellent commodities,
and our guarantee to customers is clear:
we promise you the goods are highest quality,
you won't be disappointed if you enter here.'
Oh, no, you won't be disappointed here!

(*Enter Guo Hua.*)

GUO HUA. (*Sings*)

I did but see my lady sweet,
then lost all wish to sleep or eat.
Her eyebrows newly pencilled fine,
her face adorned with all delicacy,
oh could I only make her mine,
and climb love's peak of ecstasy!

(*Says*)

If love be our destiny in any case,
a thread draws lovers together though a thousand miles
 away;
Without such destiny, though we be face to face,
we find we've not a single word to say.
If I can twine in love with her,
as the rose with the columbine,
then it shall not have been in vain,
this little life of mine.

I'm Guo Hua from Luoyang, and I've come here to Changan to take the imperial examinations. But – surprise, surprise – I discover that the date for the examinations is still a good way off, so I've been idling around the town all day and every day. The other day in Embroidery Alley I saw a cosmetics shop open, and there were a mother and her daughter inside. The mother can have been no more than fifty or so, and looked like the wife of a shopkeeper. But her daughter was a real smasher, and very refined into the bargain, with charming manners. From the look of her, she was only fifteen or sixteen. Just those two eyes of hers – let alone all the rest of her! – were enough to captivate you, enchain your soul! I couldn't very well approach her openly, and declare what I felt in so many words, so all I could do was spend the whole day going in and out on the pretext of buying rouge. I teased her and bantered with her a bit, and you could see she'd fully grasped my message. But what could I do? Her mother was around, so I couldn't start any fun and games with her. If I could see her when her mother wasn't in the vicinity, you can bet your life we could hit it off splendidly together. Must pop round there again now. My luck may be in this time, and her mother won't be there! (*Sings*)

> A short walk brings me to the streets and shops,
> and now I stride along the main high-road,
> through a little alley, and here we are
> in the quarter where stands that someone's abode.
> And far off in the distance I can spy
> that capital-style shop sign swinging high.

(*Enter Moon Bloom.*)

MOON BLOOM. Well my mother still hasn't come back. (*Sits, half smiling, behind the counter.*)

GUO HUA. Aha, marvellous! Still some way off yet, but I can see that young lady leaning so gracefully against the counter there. What a charming figure she has! (*Sings*)

> I bitterly wish, ah, would I could
> devour her in one swallow!
> Now let me go up and bow to her,
> like a thoroughly gallant fellow,
> yes, a thoroughly gallant fellow!

(*Says*) Please accept my cordial greetings, young lady.

MOON BLOOM. (*Smiling, and returning his greeting*) Ten thousand blessings upon you, my lord.

GUO HUA. Why do I not see your dear mother here today, young lady?

MOON BLOOM. Oh! she's gone round to a relative's house.

GUO HUA. Oho! So she's gone round to a relative's house, has she?

MOON BLOOM. Yes, that's right.

GUO HUA. (*Aside*) Aha, excellent. Heaven has kindly paved the way for me. Let's flirt with her a bit, and see how she reacts.

MOON BLOOM. Er ... why do you spend all day buying rouge, sir? What do you use it for?

GUO HUA. To be quite frank, young lady, I buy it as a present for someone!

(*Moon Bloom gives him a meaningful wink.*)

GUO HUA. (*Sings*)

> I buy your rouge, and I'll tell you why,
> – it's a present for my lady-love, the apple of my eye.

MOON BLOOM. Ooh, lovely. Ooh, and it's just the right colour!

GUO HUA. (*Smiling*) Oh, charming form and features! How may I cleave closer to your comely charms? (*Aside*) Hang on a minute. Her face and figure look heavenly, but I wonder whether she's got dainty feet or not? Ah, I know what I'll do. (*To Moon Bloom*) Ahem, young lady, previously I've only bought the ordinary rouge. This time would you be so good as to fetch me down some of the rouge on that top shelf? I hope it isn't putting you to too much trouble?

MOON BLOOM. Oh, so you want the rouge from the top shelf today, sir? No, that's no trouble at all. Just a moment, and I'll fetch it down. Quite simple. (*She stands up to reach for it.*)

GUO HUA. (*Watching with delight*) Phew! Aha! Wonderful! Just look at those exquisitely dainty feet!

(*Moon Bloom brings down the rouge, and hands it to Guo Hua. They clasp each other's hands.*)

GUO HUA. Hey now, this really is different from what I got the other day! (*They make eyes at each other.*) My dear young lady, there is a little something that I would like, if I may, to tell you. I wonder if you might perhaps grant me leave to do so?

MOON BLOOM. If there's something you want to say, sir, surely there's nothing to stop you.

GUO HUA. (*Sings*)
    When I see your fair features of paradise,
    I think it would be awfully nice
    if we retired somewhere and settled down, and ...

(*Stops.*)

MOON BLOOM. Oh, tired? You want to settle down? Oh please, sit down on this chair over here.

GUO HUA. No, no, not that ... (*Sings*)
    I mean, me to be the groom ...

(*Shuts up.*)

MOON BLOOM. Oh, I see, sir scholar, you don't want to settle down like that! Silly of me ... you want to settle down as a groom? What sort of groom, I wonder: a donkey groom, a horse groom, or a camel groom?

GUO HUA. No, no, not that! ... (*Sings*)
    I mean, me the groom, and you the bride.

MOON BLOOM. (*Laughs*) Oh, you're rather forthright!

GUO HUA.
    (*Sings*) Let's settle down, let's snuggle down inside,
    me as your loving groom, and you as the blushing bride!

(*They both laugh. Guo Hua leaps behind the counter to join her.*)

ITINERANT SALESMAN. (*Backstage*) Everything under the sun for sale!

MOON BLOOM. It's no good. Someone's coming.

GUO HUA. What can we do now, then?

MOON BLOOM. Never mind, just hide behind the counter for a bit.

(*Enter salesman.*)

SALESMAN. Knick-knacks, novelties, soft goods and sundries, all kinds of goods for sale! (*Sings*)

> North and south, I'm famous everywhere,
> Every kind of merchandise I bear,
> goods from Suzhou, and from Hangzhou, too,
> the very latest fashion, and all brand new.
> Toothbrushes, caskets of perfume,
> girdles for ladies' hips,
> all manner of powder and cosmetics,
> rouge for ladies' cheeks and lips.

Well, well, another little stretch of the road, and where do we find ourselves but inside of Mistress Wang's emporium! Mistress Wang!

MOON BLOOM. Ah, the haberdasher.

SALESMAN. Would you be liking to buy a girdle now, Mistress Wang?

MOON BLOOM. Not really.

SALESMAN. Well, if that's not to your liking, what would you say to buying a trumpet for a little tootle on?

MOON BLOOM. I don't need one.

SALESMAN. Well, surely you'd be eager to buy a couple of boxes of powder?

MOON BLOOM. Nor that.

SALESMAN. Well, I never! Are you not going to oblige me in any fashion whatsoever, then? Well, I have here a mirror. What say you to exchanging it for a little rouge, now?

MOON BLOOM. Nor that, either.

SALESMAN. Come now, it's a splendid bronze mirror!

(*He takes out the mirror, and looks into it. Guo Hua stands up, and Moon Bloom pushes him down again.*)

SALESMAN. Well, ain't that marvellous! What a priceless treasure of a magical mirror!

MOON BLOOM. What's priceless or magic about it?

SALESMAN. Why, there's just the two of us here in the shop, but the mirror showed us with three heads between us. Now isn't that magic? Is it not indeed!

(*Moon Bloom becomes all blushing and embarrassed.*)

SALESMAN. (*Turning his head round, away from the mirror, to have a look*) What the − ! Clear as I stand here, I saw three heads, so why the dickens are there only two folk to be found? Now isn't that something to put you in a pother!

(*He looks into the mirror again. Guo Hua stands up again, but Moon Bloom pushes him down.*)

SALESMAN. (*Aside*) Well I never! Now that face is not unknown to me. It reminds me of Guo Hua. The young bastard! Coming here today intent on a slice of frolic and fun, is he? ... Since you won't oblige me with your custom, Mistress Wang, I'll be borrowing the space in front of your shop to set out my stall and do a few penceworth of business for myself. (*Sets out goods.*)

MOON BLOOM. Oh dear! No, go and set up your stall somewhere else!

SALESMAN. It'll be all right here.

MOON BLOOM. But I don't want you to set up your stall here. I *don't want* you to!

SALESMAN. All right then, no need to get het up. I'll be on my way, then. That's all there is to it.

MOON BLOOM. Yes, and hurry up about it!

SALESMAN. (*Gathering up his wares*) Yes, yes, I'm going straight away. (*Makes as if to exit.*)

MOON BLOOM. He's gone now. You'd better hurry off quickly, too!

(*Guo Hua leaps out. Salesman intercepts and bumps into him.*)

SALESMAN. Aha, aha!

GUO HUA. I've got three pieces of silver here.

SALESMAN. What for?

GUO HUA. To pay you for not opening your mouth.

SALESMAN. Aha! (*Takes the silver and looks at it. Guo Hua snatches a girdle from him. Exit Guo Hua.*)

SALESMAN. Tut, tut, hey, hey! (*Laughs*) Huh, a mighty clever girdle that was, to get itself sold for three whole pieces of silver. Well, I might never have had them, so I might as well go and exchange them for a spot of romance. Mistress Wang, I have here three pieces of silver, so how about getting together for a cuddle and you-know-what.

MOON BLOOM. Tcha! You old swine! What do you think you're saying?

(*Enter Guo Hua.*)

GUO HUA. (*To salesman*) Hey, what are you doing in there?

SALESMAN. Aha, ehee, you see, I've got three pieces of silver here, too.

GUO HUA. What for?

SALESMAN. Well, for paying someone who won't open their mouth. (*Exit.*)

(*Moon Bloom shuts the door.*)

GUO HUA. Open the door, young lady.

MOON BLOOM. What do you want now?

GUO HUA. I forgot something, left it in your shop.

MOON BLOOM. You didn't.

GUO HUA. Open the door, so that I can come in and have a look for it.

MOON BLOOM. This door is staying shut.

GUO HUA. If you won't open up, all right! – I've got a girdle here that I've just stolen, and I'll hang myself from your doorway.

MOON BLOOM. You won't die if you do it like that.

GUO HUA. You can sometimes die even if your veins are only constricted. You can never tell ... All right then, I'm going to hang myself really then!

MOON BLOOM. You won't die if you do it that way, either.

GUO HUA. Eh, are you sure I won't that way either? All right, just you watch now. If one dies before the peony one loves most, one becomes a dashing lady-killer ghost! (*Suspends himself properly.*)

MOON BLOOM. Oh dear! He really has hung himself up now. What if mother comes back? What on earth could I say? I'd better open the door and help him down, to save his life. They say, 'Saving the life of one human being is better than building a seven-storey pagoda!'

(*Opens door. Guo Hua kisses her on the lips.*)

MOON BLOOM. Pah, how can you be so improper!

GUO HUA. Well then, what would you say if we knelt down and made our marriage vows to Heaven?

MOON BLOOM. Pooh!

(*Guo Hua drags Moon Bloom down, and they both kneel with their heads down, head to head, to perform the ceremony. Enter salesman.*)

SALESMAN. Hey, hey! They're at it again. Let's have a little fun with them now. (*He gets down with Moon Bloom, behind her. Sniffs.*)

MOON BLOOM. (*Completes her vows, rises, and sees salesman.*) Oh dear, what's that old fellow doing still here.

(*Exit Moon Bloom in a panic.*)

(*Guo Hua also finishes his vows. He rises, flings his arms around the salesman, and plants a kiss on his mouth.*)

SALESMAN. Saucepot! Gracious me – me with my mouth covered in white whiskers, and you still want to kiss me!

GUO HUA. (*Seeing salesman, drops his hands, utterly abashed*) Agh, help! (*Exit, hand over mouth.*)

SALESMAN. Tut, tut, tut! Haw, haw, ha, ha! You'd never credit it! Fancy my luck, getting involved in that sort of queer lark at my age! (*Reels off.*)

Hegemon King says farewell to his queen

Peking Opera: version by Mei Lanfang (1894–1961)

Characters:

FOUR HAN SOLDIERS: each representing an army.
CAO CAN: a Han general.
YING BU: a Han general.
KONG XI: a Han general.
CHEN HE: a Han general.
PENG YUE: a Han general.
WANG LING: a Han general.
ZHOU BO: a Han general.
FAN KUAI: a Han general.
CHEN PING: a Han general.
HAN XIN: Field Marshal of the Han forces.
Four ROYAL GUARDS of Xiang Yu.
Four MINOR EUNUCHS in the service of Xiang Yu.
Two GRAND EUNUCHS in the service of Xiang Yu.
XIANG YU: Hegemon King of Chu, the Great King.
XIANG BO: an uncle and general of Xiang Yu's, historically a traitor to his cause, and favourable to the Han.
LI ZUOCHE: a Han minister, a military strategist of renown.
YU ZIQI: a general in the service of Xiang Yu.
ZHOU LAN: a general in the service of Xiang Yu.
ZHONGLI MEI: a general in the service of Xiang Yu.
Eight PALACE MAIDS in the service of Queen Yu.
QUEEN YU: beautiful wife of Xiang Yu.
Four CHU SOLDIERS: each representing an army, in service of Xiang Yu.
FEMALE CHARIOTEER: in the service of Queen Yu.
EQUERRY: in the service of Xiang Yu.
LIU BANG: King of Han, future founder of the Han dynasty.
Four WATCHMEN in the service of Xiang Yu.
SCOUT: in the service of Xiang Yu.
MIN ZIQI: adherent of the Han, disguised as fisherman.
LÜ MATONG: a Han officer, formerly a close friend and comrade of Xiang Yu.

Scene One

(Enter four Han soldiers and Cao Can, Ying Bu, Kong Xi, Chen He, Peng

111

Yue, Wang Ling, Zhou Bo, Fan Kuai and Chen Ping, followed by Han Xin.)

HAN XIN. From my tent of war I direct and I plan,
 commanding this cock-bold host,
 and with this heart, loyal to the core, I uphold the Han.
 By Nine Mile Mountain[1] ten ambushes I have laid;
 my strategy ensures that victory is won,
 I spring forth like some spirit, I vanish like a ghost!

  I have 'mounted the stage', appointed Field-Marshal, the
   tally of command in my hand,
 My tactics and stratagems surpass Sun's and Wu's[2], my
   schemes are more cunning, my ruses more clever,
 and now I make ready in just one battle to wipe out Western
   Chu,
 to secure ten thousand miles of land; such is my bold and
   mighty endeavour.

I am Han Xin, Field-Marshal of the Han forces. I have been ordered by my monarch to assume overall command of his infantry and cavalry in a joint effort to destroy Western Chu. Ah, to think that during these last five years, since our army marched forth from Baozhong[3]; I have personally fought over seventy battles with King Xiang, coaxing my men, egging them on to further efforts, undergoing countless weary hardships and bitter sufferings. But now King Xiang is isolated and his power enfeebled, and for him it is a case of victory this time or utter ruin. Chen Ping! Hear my command.

CHEN PING. At your service.

HAN XIN. Lead your men to cut off King Xiang's retreat. There must be no mistake.

CHEN PING. Command received! (*Exit.*)

HAN XIN. Fan Kuai! Hear my command.

FAN KUAI. At your service.

HAN XIN. You bear the main flag of command in the centre of the army.

FAN KUAI. Command received!

HAN XIN. My generals one and all!

ALL. Aye.

HAN XIN. Set your forces in motion and proceed to Nine Mile Mountain.

ALL. Command received!

(*Exeunt together.*)

Scene Two

(*Enter four royal guards, four minor eunuchs and two grand eunuchs, followed by Xiang Yu.*)

XIANG YU. (*Sings*)
    Behold a great hero bold,
    no rival on this Earth to match me!
    I destroyed the Qin of the Yings[4],
    restored Chu to its territory,
    and now war throughout the world to hold the mastery.
    (*Recites*)
    Qin, of the House of Ying, wickedly waged war,
    it annexed the Six States[5], but they divided once again;
    Xiang Yu and Liu Bang settled their border along Goose
        Ditch[6],
    Han held the east and Chu held the west, where I, supreme
        hegemon, reign.
I am the Hegemon King, Xiang Yu. I and Liu Bang took Goose Ditch as the dividing line between our domains, ceased military operations against each other, and concluded a peace, whereby I sent his father-in-law and his wife Madam Lü back to him. Little did I imagine that he would break that treaty, but now he comes once more to seek war with me. I have ordered my scouts to advance and spy out the situation, but they have not yet reported back.

XIANG BO. (*Backstage*) On we go!

(*Enter Xiang Bo.*)

XIANG BO. (*Sings*)
    Zuoche has deserted the Han, and comes to render allegiance
        and proffer obedience;
    I go to inform our Sacred and Enlightened Lord of this turn
        of great significance.
I, Xiang Bo, reverently greet my monarch. A thousand years to you, Great King.

XIANG YU. Rise.

XIANG BO. A thousand thousand years to you.

XIANG YU. What matter do you wish to communicate to me that brings you to the palace?

XIANG BO. I beg to inform you, Great King, that at this moment a strategic counsellor from the state of Zhao, Li Zuoche, who has deserted the Han, is coming here to render you allegiance. He has asked me to introduce him, and is at present outside the palace, awaiting your decree.

XIANG YU. Oho. As it happens, I am short of strategic advisers just now, so it is a fortunate coincidence that Li Zuoche has come to render allegiance. The only thing that I am afraid of is that he may just be pretending to give us allegiance, and in reality be harbouring false schemes. – Announce to him that he is to enter the palace, so that I may probe him with words to discover how genuine is his change of heart.

XIANG BO. I obey your command. – The Great King issues the edict that Li Zuoche is to enter the palace!

LI ZUOCHE. (*Backstage*) Command received! (*Enters.*)
> Boldly I burst into the tiger's den,
> to lure a dragon into the shoals!

I, Li Zuoche, a refugee, greet Your Majesty. A thousand years to you, Great King.

XIANG YU. Rise.

LI ZUOCHE. A thousand thousand years.

XIANG YU. Li Zuoche!

LI ZUOCHE. Great King?

XIANG YU. I have heard that in Qi you served as Private Secretary to Han Xin. Surely, in now suddenly deserting him and coming to give your allegiance to me, you must be attempting some deception?

LI ZUOCHE. Ah, Great King … Before that, in the old days, when I served as a minister to Zhao, the King of Zhao, not heeding my advice, ordered Chen Yu[7] to join battle with Han Xin. Chen Yu was slain by Han Xin on the banks of the River Di[8], and I, having nowhere else to perch, thereupon joined Han Xin's staff. Afterwards, when Han Xin was given the title King of Qi, he grew extremely arrogant, and whenever plans were being made he would always decide everything himself. He would never listen to the advice of his staff, nor act in accordance with their tactical plans, and a good eighty or ninety per cent of them just absconded from his service. In my own case, having heard that you, Great King, are about to join battle with Liu Bang, I am eager to place myself under your banner of command, and prove the sincerity of my adherence to you by toiling for you as would your dog or horse. Nothing could be further from my mind than deception!

XIANG YU. Huh. When two countries engage in battle, false surrenders are very frequent. You must certainly be coming here now with the aim of spying out how substantial my forces are!

LI ZUOCHE. Oh, Great King, in speaking thus you speak in error. I'm just a strategic adviser, you know, incapable of donning tough armour or of wielding a keen blade, nor any good at spearheading attacks on the enemy. I shall merely accompany you, as one of your attendants, and assist you with logistical and strategical planning. Whether you heed my counsel or not will be entirely up to Your Great Majesty. As for the substantiality of the Chu camp, Han Xin is constantly receiving reports from his scouts, and does not need my false surrender before he can know of such things. If you entertain suspicions of me, Great King, it means that I have lacked noble insight in turning to the wrong ruler, and that I have lacked wisdom in leaving myself thus adrift and helpless. The best thing then that I can do is die here before you, Great King, and thereby render the true inclinations of my heart manifest beyond all doubt.

(*Makes to dash himself to death.*)

XIANG YU. Hold on! (*Laughs*) Ha ha ha ... I was just joking with you. Your outstanding reputation has long been known to me, Venerable Versed-in-war, and in days gone by I was once going to go to the Kingdom of Zhao and engage your services so that you might do my tactical planning. Now that you have come over to me of your own true will, I must day and night discuss with you what schemes we can find for defeating the Han.

LI ZUOCHE. If you think fit to keep me here, Great King, I shall be ready to give my life to prove my worth, Your Majesty.

XIANG YU. A true and worthy statesman to uphold the altars of my kingdom!

YU ZIQI *and* ZHOU LAN. (*Backstage*) Come on!

(*Enter Yu Ziqi and Zhou Lan together.*)

YU ZIQI. (*Sings*)
 From the province of Wu the men of Kuaiji come speeding,
ZHOU LAN. (*Sings*)
 But Zhou Yin sets at naught his monarch's beck and bidding.
YU ZIQI *and* ZHOU LAN. We greet Your Majesty. A thousand years to you, Great King.
XIANG YU. Rise, my two lords.
YU ZIQI *and* ZHOU LAN. A thousand thousand years.
XIANG YU. What words have you for your king?
ZHOU LAN. I beg to inform you, Great King, that, as you previously ordered, Lin Ning went to Kuaiji to arrange the transfer of forces. The moment the Governor received your summons, he that very same day mobilized his troops, which are advancing to aid you in this war. Then we proceeded to Shu and Liu[9], to fetch Zhou Yin's forces here, but alas, it was no use, for Zhou Yin in contravention

of Your Majesty's command holds his men in check and makes no move. I beg Your Majesty to determine what steps should now be taken.

XIANG YU. Ah! The impudence of Zhou Yin, to dare to disobey my orders! I vow I shall first destroy that scoundrel, even before I crush Han.

XIANG BO. Wait a minute. I beg to make a submission to you, Great King. In view of the fact that Zhou Yin is no more of an affliction than a rash on the skin, while Liu Bang is a grave malady that strikes at heart and belly, I would beg Your Great Majesty to think, think, and think again.

XIANG YU. Let me ponder over the matter.

(*Enter Zhongli Mei.*)

ZHONGLI MEI. I beg to inform you, Great King, that Han Xin has posted up a notice insulting and reviling Your Great Majesty. I have taken a careful copy of its wording, which I invite Your Majesty to read.

XIANG YU. Submit your copy to me. Now, let me peruse it:
    'In the cause of honour the princes join
    to haul the wicked villain in.
    People's hearts all turn from Chu in disaffection,
    and Heaven gives Liu of the Flame[10] its favour and protection.
    One day soon, at Borderfoot[11] ruined he shall lie,
    we near the hour when at Pei Bower[12] he will die.
    Fierce fire blazing from the flash of our sword,
    we shall slice off King Xiang's ear[13] and chop off his head.'
Tcha, ya, ya …. (*Sings*)
    Through clenched teeth I blast Han Xin with bitter curses,
    when I catch that scoundrel, I shall cut him in a thousand
        slices.
My lords and ministers all, transmit for me this decree of mine: this very day we shall unleash our armies and smash Han.

ZHOU LAN. Wait a minute. I beg to submit to you, Great King, that it is because Han Xin fears that Your Majesty will keep his forces in check and not stir from his positions that he has uttered these frenzied words, in an attempt to provoke you to hasty wrath. If, Great King, you send your troops forth, it is certain that you will be falling for some trick of Han Xin's to lure them into a trap. Think it over, Great King, think and think again.

XIANG YU. But my lord, in my travels throughout the world I have never once endured an insult for as long as one single day. Now that this common knave thus insults and vilifies me, if I just hold my forces in check and make no move, I'll render myself the

shameful laughing-stock of all the monarchs on earth, won't I!
YU ZIQI. I beg to submit to you, Great King, that Han has come in
great military force, and that, furthermore, Han Xin is full of wily
ruses. In my foolish opinion, the only course to adopt is to deepen
our moats, heighten our fortifications, and for the time being take
no military initiative, but wait till their armies are weary and
exhausted. At that point Your Majesty, by thus biding in leisure
while the enemy toils, will be able to drum your men forward,
advance westwards, and, in but one battle, gain the victory. This
way will afford Han Xin no chance of deploying his stratagems,
and will prevent Zhang Liang [14] from accomplishing any tactical
plans. And then you will be able to take Yingyang[15] and
Chenggao[16] as easy as spitting on your hand.
XIANG YU. I ... er ...
LI ZUOCHE. Oh no, Great King, if you do not attack, and lead the
campaign yourself in person, the Han forces are bound to attack
Pengcheng[17], and if it fails to hold out, Your Great Majesty will no
longer have any home to return to. The best thing to do would be
to take active command of your troops and personally lead them
into battle. Then, if you prove victorious, you will be in a position
to destroy the Han forces, while if you fail to gain the victory you
can withdraw back to Pengcheng. Such a plan of action leaves you
free to advance and do battle or to withdraw and carry out a
successful defence. You would surely be most mistaken to discard
such a sound tactical plan in preference to 'watching the tree-
stump'![18]
XIANG YU. Hmmm. Your suggestion, Venerable Sir, very much
coincides with my own inclinations. – My ministers! All of you are
to convey this decree of mine: this very day we shall march
forward and defeat Han.
YU ZIGI. I would still like to implore you, Great King, to think again
and again.
XIANG YU. My mind is already made up. There is no need to proffer
me any further counsel on the matter. – Ah, yes, indeed, now that
I have obtained your services, Venerable Sir, I am bound to gain
the upper hand and secure the victory.
ALL. This very day we march forward to destroy the Han forces!

(*Exeunt all, except Yu Ziqi, separately.*)

YU ZIQI. Just a minute, now ... ! As I see things, there is something
not quite genuine about Li Zuoche's coming here. But the Great
King has already determined that he will march his troops forth,
and we cannot prevent him, so what on earth is to be done? Ah, I
have it! I must go into the palace seraglio, and have a talk about

things with Her Majesty. Perhaps she may be able to prevent the Great King from marching his troops out. You can never tell. Yes, yes:

> In the Golden Hall I cannot alter my monarch's decision,
> so must beg Her Majesty to work her persuasion.

(*Exit.*)

Scene Three

(*Enter eight palace maids bearing tallies and holding fans, followed by Queen Yu.*)

QUEEN YU.

> No more does the Toad Light[19] moon shine bright,
> and in the golden wind of autumn
> the drums and trumpets sound forth bleak and desolate.
>
> I think and wonder, since first I travelled to theatres of war,
> how many years have run, how many times the frost of
>   winter has fallen, the planets have spun!
> Ah, when, if ever, will my prayer be answered? When shall I
>   see home again?
> And when will the vapours of war melt away into tranquil
>   moonlight and radiant sun?

I am Queen Yu, in the retinue of the Hegemon King of Western Chu. I was born and grew up in secluded boudoirs, but, when a child, became thoroughly acquainted with the arts of calligraphy and swordsmanship. Since I bound myself to the Great King, I have been through campaigns and wars all over the world, enduring great hardship and arduous toil. I wonder if I will ever know an age of real peace!

(*Enter Yu Ziqi.*)

YU ZIQI.

> In haste I bear news of the war situation
> for her Majesty's consideration.

Here I am now in the royal seraglio. Let me knock at the ring.
PALACE MAID. Who is it knocking at the ring?
YU ZIQI. Yu Ziqi requests an audience.
PALACE MAID. Wait there.
YU ZIQI. Certainly.
PALACE MAID. I beg to inform Your Majesty that Yu Ziqi is seeking an audience with you.

QUEEN YU. Convey my permission to him to enter the seraglio.

PALACE MAID. Yes, ma'am. – Yu Ziqi is to enter the seraglio!

YU ZIQI. I obey the command. – I, Yu Ziqi, greet our queen. A thousand years to you, Your Majesty.

QUEEN YU. Rise.

YU ZIQI. A thousand thousand years.

QUEEN YU. What business brings you into the seraglio?

YU ZIQI. I ... there is a host of eyes and ears present.

QUEEN YU. (*To palace maids*) Withdraw, all of you.

EIGHT PALACE MAIDS. Certainly, ma'am. (*Exeunt maids, separately.*)

QUEEN YU. What important matter have you that requires such urgency and secrecy?

YU ZIQI. I beg to submit to Your Majesty that at this moment Liu Bang, Han Xin and others, in command of great forces, are advancing to seek battle with us. Numerically our forces are no match for theirs, and the proper thing for us to do would be to deepen our moats, heighten our fortifications, and sit back at our leisure until they exhaust themselves. But, alas, the Great King is heeding the suggestions of the renegade minister Li Zuoche, and has issued the decree that our men are to march out and advance against the enemy tomorrow. I only fear that if we do so now, the Great King will prove the victim of someone's ruse.

QUEEN YU. Why did all the ministers not remonstrate with him, and try to stop him?

YU ZIQI. His ministers attempted several times to dissuade him, but he would not heed them.

QUEEN YU. What is to be done, then?

YU ZIQI. I would like to ask Your Majesty to make another attempt, to try and persuade the Great King that on no account whatsoever must he send forth his soldiers.

QUEEN YU. Well then, retire for a while, my lord, and when the Great King returns to the seraglio let me try to dissuade him from such an action.

YU ZIQI. I am most grateful, Your Majesty. (*Exit.*)

QUEEN YU. But wait a minute. Just now I heard Ziqi's view that it would be to our grave disadvantage to move our troops out and to give battle. But what can I do? The Great King has a fierce and stubborn nature, and will not adopt sincere advice. I fear that some day he will surely suffer at the hands of the Han forces. The very thought of such a thing fills me with anxiety!

(*Enter eight palace maids, unobtrusively.*)

QUEEN YU. (*Sings*)

    His Majesty the Great King is headstrong and wilful,

and often refuses to heed well-meant and loyal counsel.
My fear is that others will seize the land of Western Chu,
setting at nought his fearsome fame for a dozen years and
more of mighty mettle.

(*Enter four royal guardsmen and two grand eunuchs, followed by Xiang Yu.*)

XIANG YU. (*Sings*)
In my acquiring Li Zuoche the Kingdom of Chu met with a
lucky chance.
I go to the seraglio to counsel with my royal Lady about my
forces' imminent advance.
QUEEN YU. Ah, Great King.
XIANG YU. My royal Lady.

(*Exeunt, unobtrusively, four royal guardsmen and two grand eunuchs.*)

QUEEN YU. Your humble lady welcomes her monarch. A thousand
years to you, Great King!
XIANG YU. Rise, my royal Lady.
QUEEN YU. A thousand thousand years to you.
XIANG YU. You may be seated.
QUEEN YU. I thank you.
XIANG YU. Most annoying, most annoying!
QUEEN YU. Great King! Why, when you return to the seraglio
today, are you so vexed?
XIANG YU. Ah, little do you know why, my royal Lady! At this very
hour Liu Bang, with all the other rulers he has gathered around
him, is mobilizing his troops and advancing towards us in order to
make war on me. He has, furthermore, distributed many public
notices vilifying your solitary monarch. Don't you think I've good
cause to be vexed?
QUEEN YU. Great King, you should deepen your moats, heighten
your fortifications, and wait for relief forces. Otherwise, I fear that
we are too few to match their hordes, and shall indeed fall victim
to one of their number's stratagems.
XIANG YU. But, you see, that Liu Bang is such a fickle and
perfidious fellow, and that Han Xin is so treacherous and sly! This
time I march my men out to battle, I am determined to seize Han
Xin, and to eliminate Liu Bang. Nothing less will vent the
bitterness that rages within me!
QUEEN YU. It is a vital principle in conducting any military
operations to know yourself and to know others. If, because of
some wrath of the moment, you lose self-control, I'm afraid that,
what with the overwhelming numerical strength of the Han
forces, and Han Xin's wiliness, good fortune will not bless you,

Great King. In my worthless opinion, you should resort to solid defensive tactics, and utterly avoid any capricious initiatives. Look well before you leap, Great King!

XIANG YU. Although your advice is sound, my royal Lady, if I fail to go forth and do battle I shall without doubt become the laughing-stock of all the monarchs in the world!

QUEEN YU. Only a man of mettle but flexible as situations demand can ever be a true hero. And there is no fear of anybody mocking such a man!

XIANG YU. Oh ... ! – Ach! I'm going to do battle, and I swear that this time I shall never turn back until I have destroyed Han. You must not submit any more advice to me on the matter, my royal Lady.

QUEEN YU. If your mind is already made up, Great King, I would not dare to offer you any further advice. In that case, then, on what day shall you go out to do battle?

XIANG YU. We march forth tomorrow. You, royal Lady, shall accompany me.

QUEEN YU. As you command. I pray that in this campaign, Great King, wherever your flag unfurls you may obtain victory, and wherever your horse gallops you may meet with success. I shall prepare wine, and we shall have a drink beforehand, a little party together.

XIANG YU. I am grateful that you go to such trouble for me, my royal Lady. (*Sings*)

> I only pray that this time, wherever my flag unfurls, ours may
> be the victory,

QUEEN YU. (*Sings*)

> Destroy Liu Bang and seize Han Xin, that we together may
> enjoy rich peace and tranquillity.

(*Exeunt all, together.*)

Scene Four

(*Enter Xiang Bo, Zhou Lan, Yu Ziqi and Zhongli Mei, one after the other, making the gestures and postures of adjusting their helmets and buckling on their armour, then standing in the front centre of the stage and lifting their sleeves in front of their face in a customary indication that they are embarking upon military action.*)

ALL FOUR GENERALS. We are:

XIANG BO. Xiang Bo,
ZHOU LAN. Zhou Lan,
YU ZIQI. Yu Ziqi,
ZHONGLI MEI. and Zhongli Mei.
XIANG BO. Greetings, generals.
OTHER THREE GENERALS. Greetings.
XIANG BO. The Great King has commanded us to muster the troops, and all are now assembled. Gazing into the far far distance, I see ...
OTHER THREE GENERALS. Here comes the Great King.

(*Enter four Chu soldiers, four royal guardsmen, Li Zuoche, Queen Yu, female charioteer, equerry, and Xiang Yu, together.*)

XIANG YU.
    As unrivalled generals the whole world knows us,
    such is our fame, who dares oppose us?
ALL GENERALS. Our reverent greetings to you, Great King.
XIANG YU. Are all the troops assembled and in order?
ALL GENERALS. Aye, they are all assembled and in order.
XIANG YU. Forward towards the battle!
ALL GENERALS. (*Conveying the command*) Forward to the battle!
ALL. Aye.

(*Exeunt soldiers and generals, and Queen Yu and female charioteer, together. Xiang Yu circles the stage, holding out his horse-whip, to signify that he is riding off. The main flag of command which is being held by the equerry is snapped in two by the wind*).

EQUERRY. The wind is so wild it has snapped the grand flag of command in two.
XIANG YU. Ah, curse it! (*Sings*)
    In a trice the wild-gusting wind wreaks havoc,
    what does it mean by snapping in twain my flag of
        command?
    And my Raven Dapple snorts and whinnies all the while ...

(*Horse neighs. Xiang Yu reins in his horse in alarm.*)

XIANG YU. Hey! ...... (*Sings*)
    his whole body's a-tremble, and his neigh rings out across the
        wide land.
(*Says*) Turn the men back!

(*Enter all, together, turning back along their tracks.*)

ALL. Why are you ordering your troops back, Great King?

XIANG YU. No sooner had I sent them forth than a wild wind snapped the grand flag of command in two, and my charger began neighing loudly. Now why should that be?

ZHOU LAN. I beg to submit to you, Great King, that the flag's snapping and the horse's neighing bode ill for our army. Think carefully, Great King.

XIANG YU. (*Disagreeing*) Huh! Wicked King Zhou[20] fell and good King Wu[21] rose on one and the same day. Why should I take my cue from the former and not from the latter! What has the flag's snapping and my horse's neighing to do with our army's advance?

QUEEN YU. I beg to proffer an opinion, Great King. My lord Zhou Lan here is a minister of proven loyalty to you, and you must not ignore his advice. I would truly consider myself infinitely blessed with good fortune were you to follow good counsel and heed loyal advice concerning today's campaign, as indeed you must!

XIANG YU. I ... er ...

LI ZUOCHE. Oh, Great King, a thousand times no! Nay, ten thousand times no! You must not withdraw your troops. I have heard that the Han forces are short of provisions. As soon as you approach them with your mighty army, Your Great Majesty, they will fall apart in confusion before it even comes to fighting. You must not lose this opportunity, Great King.

XIANG YU. Mm! Your advice, Venerable Sir, completely coincides with my own views on the matter. Now, convey my command: our main force is to advance towards Pei province[22].

LI ZUOCHE. Advance towards Pei province!

(*Exeunt all, together. Li Zuoche, however, slips back again.*)

LI ZUOCHE. Not so fast! Now, thank goodness, I have got Xiang Yu to fall for my trick, and my noble deed is accomplished, so all that remains is for me to return to my camp and report to Field Marshal Han Xin. (*Exit.*)

Scene Five

(*Enter four Chu soldiers, four royal guardsmen, Zhongli Mei, Yu Ziqi, Zhou Lan, Xiang Bo, female charioteer, equerry and Xiang Yu, all together. All cease their advance.*)

XIANG YU. Why have you stopped?

ALL. We have reached Pei province.

XIANG YU. Pitch camp and secure the palisades!

(All go round the stage. Enter scout.)

SCOUT. Reporting! Han Xin is drilling his men at Nine Mile Mountain. They are in excellent shape, and have plenty of provisions. That is what I have to report.

XIANG YU. Go and reconnoitre once more.

SCOUT. I obey your command. *(Exit.)*

XIANG YU. Eh? ... The scout reported that Han Xin's troops were in excellent shape, and had plenty of provisions, yet Li Zuoche told me the Han forces lacked provisions. He must surely have come to deceive me!

QUEEN YU. Summon Li Zuoche, and question him.

XIANG YU. Li Zuoche is to enter my command tent!

XIANG BO. Li Zuoche! Li Zuoche! – I beg to submit, Great King, that Li Zuoche has disappeared.

XIANG YU. What a scoundrel! *(Sings)*

 Zuoche came to join us, bent on this cunning treachery,
(Says) Xiang Bo! *(Sings)*

 You introduced him: how can you deny your crime or avoid
 the penalty?

Tcha! You rash fellow, Xiang Bo, not to investigate Li Zuoche's motives for joining us, but to introduce him and recommend him to me without any hesitation! All the guilt for my being led into such grave errors in such an important enterprise lies with you!

XIANG BO. I humbly confess, Great King, that I did wrong to recommend Li Zuoche when he came and feigned allegiance, and that the guilt for this crime is truly mine. I only beg Your Great Majesty to show lenience and forgive me.

XIANG YU. Huh! I pardon you provisionally, to give you the chance to show me how you can redeem yourself in action.

XIANG BO. I thank you, Great King.

XIANG YU. Pah! How I repent that I ignored the advice of my generals and my royal Lady, and allowed myself to fall for the sly rogue's ruse!

QUEEN YU. Never mind what I said. It's not worth consideration. I hope and am sure that now, Great King, you will arouse your valiant ire, go forth into battle, and swiftly accomplish your mighty enterprise, so that I may share in your yet greater glory and good fortune.

XIANG YU. Go and rest in the inner tent, my royal Lady.

QUEEN YU. I obey your command. *(Exit.)*

XIANG YU. My officers, all of you!

ALL. Aye!

XIANG YU. Attack!

(All go round the stage. Enter four Han soldiers, and Cao Can, Ying Bu, Kong Xi, Chen He, Peng Yue, Wang Ling, Zhou Bo, Fan Kuai, and Liu Bang, together. The two sides enter from opposite sides of the stage and station themselves there, signifying that they are drawn up to meet each other in battle.)

LIU BANG. Greetings, Xiang Yu.

XIANG YU. Liu Bang! Last time, when I defeated you at Guling [23], I spared your life, and these five years past I have never once clashed with you in personal combat. But today we must indeed see which of us is greater in prowess.

LIU BANG. Xiang Yu, I fight you in wit and not in valour. And today, I guarantee that in this one battle I shall destroy your whole army.

XIANG YU. Balderdash, every word you say! Taste my spear!

(Fan Kuai intercepts Xiang Yu. Exeunt four Han soldiers, Liu Bang, four Chu soldiers, four royal guardsmen, and four Chu generals, separately. The eight Han generals engage Xiang Yu in combat, then exeunt Han generals, feigning defeat.)

XIANG YU. After them!

(Enter four Chu soldiers, four royal guardsmen and four Chu generals, together. They cross the stage together, and exeunt in pursuit. Exit Xiang Yu in pursuit.)

Scene Six

(Enter four Han soldiers, eight Han generals, Li Zuoche and Liu Bang, together. They rush into a mountain pass, and exeunt together. Enter four Chu soldiers, four royal guardsmen, four Chu generals, and Xiang Yu, together.)

XIANG YU. Wait now! See that mountain pass ahead. That fellow Liu Bang must have fled into the mountains. – My generals!

ALL. Aye.

XIANG YU. Follow me in pursuit of him.

XIANG BO. Not so fast. The rogue may be playing some trick to lure our forces into a trap. Don't fall for it!

XIANG YU. Ah! ... *(Sings)*

> One word from him is enough to put me on my guard once
>   more,
> I fear some trap, some trick to lead us on, some cunning lure.
> Cease the advance, convey my command: our troops must
>   now withdraw!

ALL. Aye!

(All withdraw their troops, turn round, and exeunt. Enter Li Zuoche unobtrusively, onto the top of a crag.)

LI ZUOCHE. Turn again, I beg you, Great King!

(Xiang Yu reins in his horse, and turns his head round to look back.)

LI ZUOCHE. Great King! *(Sings)*
    Your Majesty, I have a little suggestion for your ear!
(Says) Great King! The House of Han is in the ascendancy, and the Kingdom of Chu is now doomed to destruction. You have already entered the cage-trap, Great King, so why not, while you still have the chance, surrender and render us your allegiance? I shall gladly act as intermediary for you. Think about it, Great King. Look before you leap any further.

XIANG YU. Who is it addressing me?

LI ZUOCHE. Li Zuoche speaking.

XIANG YU. You vile knave! Luring me out here to do battle! I bitterly wish I could smash your corpse into smithereens. Nothing less would vent my loathing for you!

LI ZUOCHE. But would you dare enter these mountains?

XIANG YU. My generals all!

ALL. *(Backstage)* Aye!

XIANG YU. After them!

(Exit Li Zuoche. Exit Xiang Yu in pursuit. Enter, together, four Chu soldiers, four royal guardsmen, Zhongli Mei, Zhou Lan, Xiang Bo, Queen Yu, female charioteer and Yu Ziqi. They cross the stage, and exeunt together in pursuit.)

Scene Seven

HAN XIN. *(Backstage, sings)*
    At the foot of Nine Mile Mountain the banners of battle fly,

(Enter four Han soldiers, Fan Kuai, grasping the great flag of command, and Han Xin, together.)

HAN XIN. *(Sings)*
    I've laid ambushes all round, and mighty deeds are nigh.
    Let us dismount, and go on foot, follow the mountain path
        up high,

    *(Han Xin dismounts from his horse, and he and the others ascend the
    mountain.)*

HAN XIN. (*Sings*)
>Where I stand aloft on the mountain, and wave my
>>signal-flag through the sky.

(*Enter eight Han generals holding flags. They draw up in battle formation. Enter Li Zuoche, followed by Xiang Yu. They enter the Han lines. Exit Li Zuoche. Exit Xiang Yu in pursuit of him. Exeunt eight Han generals, following them.*)

HAN XIN. (*Sings*)
>Li Zuoche leads King Xiang through our lines rashly
>>blundering,
>all the princes vie, in valorous union striving, great deeds
>>performing,
>fighting till the blood runs rivers, and corpses pile like
>>mountains tumbling.
>We shall destroy Western Chu and capture King Xiang Yu
>>this very morning.

XIANG YU. (*Backstage, sings*)
>On I fight, ever bolder, ferocious rage exploding from me.

(*Enter Xiang Yu. Enter eight Han generals in pursuit of him. They encircle him.*)

XIANG YU. (*Sings*)
>The men of Han bear down upon me, like a flood tide
>>surging on me.
>Where's Zhou Lan with our reserve? Where? I cannot see
>>him.

(*Enter Zhongli Mei and Zhou Lan, together.*)

ZHOU LAN. (*Sings*)
>Rescue Great King from the tiger-trap, break through and
>>quickly free him.

(*Zhongli Mei rescues Xiang Yu, and exits with him. Zhou Lan receives a thrust, and is killed. Exeunt Zhou Lan and eight Han generals, together.*)

HAN XIN. (*Sings*)
>Turn back, you men of Han, ride back now, campward wend.

(*Han Xin and the others descend from the mountain. Exeunt four Han soldiers and Fan Kuai, together.*)

HAN XIN. (*Sings*)
>I shall set another snare, with songs from Chu, their native
>>land. (*Exit.*)

Scene Eight

(*Enter eight palace maids, followed by Queen Yu.*)

QUEEN YU. (*Sings*)
> Since first I joined my Great King in his warring through the
> world,
> I have suffered frost and wind and weary toil year after year;
> Curses on wicked Qin that sent so many souls into misery's
> mire and coals,
> that crushed the common folk, brought them wretched woes
> and frantic fear.

(*Enter four royal guards and two grand eunuchs, followed by Xiang Yu.*)

XIANG YU. (*Sings*)
> Many a mighty captain from the camp of Han I pricked out
> on my spear,
> but for all my valour what could I do, ambushed on all sides,
> sore pressed!
> Tell my generals to cease the battle, all must return to their
> tents.

TWO GRAND EUNUCHS. Here comes the Great King!

(*Exit four royal guards and two grand eunuchs, separately. Queen Yu
welcomes Xiang Yu into the tent.*)

QUEEN YU. Ah, Great King, you!
XIANG YU. (*Sings*)
> This time I have brought you much alarm, wrought you
> troubled and distressed.

QUEEN YU. Oh, Great King, how did the battle go today? Was it
victory or defeat?
XIANG YU. Ah me! I pricked out many a leading general of the Han
side, but what could we do? We were helpless against their
overwhelming numbers, and we couldn't possibly have carried
the day. It is Heaven that is ruining my Chu! Ah me! For I did no
military wrong!
QUEEN YU. Soldiers always have their ups and downs. It's nothing
to worry over. I have made ready some wine, and now I shall drink
a few cups with you, Great King, to drive away your cares.
XIANG YU. Thank you for going to such trouble, my royal Lady.
QUEEN YU. (*To palace maids*) Fetch some wine.
EIGHT PALACE MAIDS. Certainly, ma'am.
XIANG YU. (*Sings*)

128

Returning today, defeated in battle, my mood is restless, all
  distraught.
QUEEN YU. (*Sings*)
  I urge you, Great King, put your mind at rest, give your
    troubles no more thought.
XIANG YU. (*Sings*)
  But the enemy lies on every side, how can reserves get
    through to aid us?
QUEEN YU. (*Sings*)
  Just have patience, keep to your lines, and wait for relieving
    forces.
XIANG YU. Oh dear, oh dear! (*Sings*)
  There's nothing I can do but drink the jewelled liquid and
    drown my cares in wine.
QUEEN YU. Great King! (*Sings*)
  The soldier has ups and downs, they've always said so, and it
    happens all the time.
XIANG YU. (*Yawns*) Awww ... !
QUEEN YU. Your limbs are weary, Great King. Why not rest awhile
within your tent?
XIANG YU. Yes, but you must wake me if need be, my royal Lady.
QUEEN YU. I shall do as you command. – Now, all of you, withdraw.
EIGHT PALACE MAIDS. Yes, ma'am.

(*Xiang Yu enters tent. Exeunt eight palace maids, separately. First watch:
Queen Yu, bearing a lamp, comes out of the tent to take a careful look round to
see that all is well, then reenters tent. Enter four nightwatchmen, separately.
They carry out the watch patrol, then exeunt, separately. Second watch.*)

QUEEN YU. My Great King is lying in his tent in a drunken sleep
there. I must go outside, and take a little stroll.
(*Sings*)
  I see the Great King, fully clothed, soundly sleeping there,
  I leave the tent to try and dispel my sorrows in the open air.
  Tiptoeing forward, until I halt in the wild, empty land, I stand
    there, still,
  and, suddenly looking up, I see in its cerulean dwelling the
    bright moon shining clear.
See the clouds withdrawing from the sky, and the Wheel of Ice
spurting high, a typical scene of autumn, sharp and pure.
ALL CHU SOLDIERS. (*Backstage*) Ah, bitter days!
QUEEN YU. A beautiful moonlit scene, to be sure, but from all sides
come the sounds of sorrow and lamentation. It makes one feel so
miserable. It is all the fault of that wicked King of Qin. Because of
him, fighting started everywhere, and poor human beings were

cast into the 'mire and coals' of suffering, a great multitude of innocent people parted from their loved ones, far separated from their father and mothers, wives deserted and children abandoned. It is impossible not to grieve bitterly over what has happened. Ah yes, indeed: 'What did they fight for, all those past heroes of mighty mettle, when all they won was their bones lying chill on the field of battle'?

(*Third watch. Enter four watchmen, and carry out the watch patrol.*)

WATCHMAN A. Did you hear that, lads?

OTHER WATCHMEN. Hear what?

WATCHMAN A. That sound, those songs the enemy troops are singing on every side of us. They've got a flavour about them the same as the tunes of our old homeland. What on earth's going on?

OTHER WATCHMEN. You're right! Wonder what on earth's going on?

WATCHMAN A. Ah, I know! It must be that Liu Bang's now occupied the land of Chu, so these soldiers he's brought here are recruits from Chu, our fellow-countrymen. That's why they're singing songs from the old country all the time. That's what it is, don't you think?

WATCHMAN B. You're right. It's terrible. What the dickens can be done now?

WATCHMAN C. Never mind. His Majesty, our Great King, will know what to do.

WATCHMAN D. Come off it! When does our lord the Great King ever have any good ideas? Apart from boozing day in day out, he hasn't the foggiest notion what to do about anything?

WATCHMAN A. Yes, you're dead right there. Our lord and master the Great King can't stand honest well-meant advice, and he's incapable of telling a good man from a bad one. He gave Li Zuoche a position, put his trust in him – inviting a wolf into his house he was – and went and fell for his trick to lure us into battle. And now he's got himself stuck in trouble here at Borderfoot, hanging on the hope day after day that troops from Chu will come to his relief. But now Liu Bang's taken the land of Chu, too, it's cut off any chances of bringing up relief forces from the rear. Oh, how the dickens are we going to get out of this mess?

(*Queen Yu eavesdrops on their conversation.*)

WATCHMAN B. If you take my advice, the lot of us ought to split up, and each make his way home as fast as he can.

WATCHMAN A. Aw, watch what twaddle you're saying! Our lord

the Great King is very stern and harsh with his military laws, and if we should chance to slip up, it doesn't bear thinking what terrible things would happen to us! What matters for us at the moment is to get on with our watch patrol!

OTHER WATCHMEN. On we go then. Keep going!

(*Fourth watch. Exeunt all the watchmen, together.*)

QUEEN YU. Oh dear, oh dear, now! I just overheard the soldiers discussing things together, and it seems that because no relief forces are reaching us everybody is inclined to desert. Oh, oh, dear me, Great King, oh, Great King! I fear you have lost the whip-hand! Things no longer go your way. (*Sings*)

Just now I heard the men all idly chatting,
and all they said showed they were for deserting.

HAN SOLDIERS. (*Backstage, singing a Chu song.*)

Your fields will be tangled with weeds: why don't you come
home?
The army takes you a thousand miles: for whose sake do you
roam?

QUEEN YU. Oh, dear, (*Sings*)

As I ponder here alone, solitary broodings sifting,
suddenly, from the enemy camp, songs of Chu come drifting.

Oh, oh, what is that now! How is it that I can hear the sound of songs from the Kingdom of Chu being sung in the enemy stockades? What can be the reason for it? There is something decidedly odd about it. I must go into the tent, and report it to my Great King. – Oh, Great King, wake up! Great King, wake up!

XIANG YU. (*Comes out of tent, alarmed*) Eh, what is it?

QUEEN YU. It is me, your lady, here.

XIANG YU. My royal Lady! What are you doing, in such a panic and alarm?

QUEEN YU. Just now I was strolling outside the camp when suddenly I heard from within the enemy stockade songs of the Kingdom of Chu, of all things! I can't imagine what it can mean!

XIANG YU. What? Is such a thing possible?

QUEEN YU. Yes, that is what is happening.

XIANG YU. Wait now, and I'll come and listen.

QUEEN YU. Yes, do, I beg you, Great King.

HAN SOLDIERS. (*Backstage, singing a Chu song*)

On the field of battle, stout knights, careless of their lives, are
slain;
from ten years in the wars campaigning, how few, how few
men ever reach home again!

XIANG YU. Oh, ah, dear, dear! ... My royal Lady! The sound of songs of the Kingdom of Chu is coming from all sides around us. Surely it cannot mean that Liu Bang has already taken the land of Chu?

QUEEN YU. There is no need for panic. Send men to spy out the truth on every side, before deliberating any further moves.

XIANG YU. That is a sensible suggestion. – Where are my personal attendants?

QUEEN YU. Where are His Majesty's personal attendants?

(*Enter two eunuchs, together.*)

TWO EUNUCHS. We reverently greet you, Great King. What are your instructions?

XIANG YU. We can hear the sound of songs of Chu from all around. My instructions are that you go and make a speedy reconnaissance, and report back to me what is happening.

TWO EUNUCHS. We obey your commands. (*Exeunt both, together.*)

XIANG YU. Huh! I feel there is something most uncanny about this business.

QUEEN YU. Let us wait and see what report your attendants will bring back.

(*Enter two eunuchs, together.*)

TWO EUNUCHS. We beg to submit to you, Great King, that it is indeed songs of the Kingdom of Chu that can be heard from the enemy camp. Such is the substance of our report.

XIANG YU. Go and make more detailed inquiries and investigations, then report back to me again.

TWO EUNUCHS. We obey your command. (*Exeunt both, together.*)

XIANG YU. My royal Lady! There are many men of Chu among the enemy forces. Liu Bang must already have taken the land of Chu. The tide of events is no longer with me!

QUEEN YU. Nowadays, with all the Central Plain torn by huntsmen vying after the 'stag' of world domination, and the powerful monarchs rising together, bold cockerels in combat, it is the normal thing occasionally to meet with setbacks. Just bide your time, wait till relief forces come from south of the Yangtse, then do battle with the enemy once more, and who can tell at whose hand the stag may then meet its death?

XIANG YU. Oh, my royal Lady, you just don't realize! Before, when the bold heroes from this region and that were warring on their own separate account, I was in a position to wipe out this place, then occupy that, one by one. But now, forces from every region have united of one accord to attack me, and stuck here at Borderfoot, with few troops and my provisions exhausted, there is absolutely no question of my being able to stay in defence. To be sure, my Eight Thousand Warrior Youths were fiercely valorous and stout in mettle, but what good is that now, when they are all scattered and gone? This time I go forth to do battle, to fight that bandit. It could go either way. There is no certainty that I shall be the victor. Ah me, alas, my royal Lady, from the look of things, the day has come for you and me to be parted.

(*Enter two grand eunuchs, unobtrusively, and separately.*)

XIANG YU. (*Sings*)
> Ten years we have cloven together in love, close in body, close in heart,
> but now the hour looms, and all too soon you and I must part.

(*Sound of horse neighing.*)

XIANG YU. Ah, there's my Raven Dapple neighing loud and clear. – Attendants, come over here.
EUNUCHS. At your service.
XIANG YU. Lead my horse Raven Dapple here to me.
EUNUCHS. Yes, Your Majesty. (*Lead horse in.*)
XIANG YU. Oh, Raven Dapple! Oh Raven Dapple! When I think how you have kept with me, warring through the world, victorious in every battle of a hundred battles. But now we are hemmed in at Borderfoot here, and even you ... Ah me, there's no room for even you to use your prowess for me now! (*Sings*)
> Even my Raven Dapple knows the tide has turned, our mastery has ebbed away,
> and by the doorway of my tent he snorts dismay,
> gives many a loud and fretful neigh!

(*Two grand eunuchs lead the horse away, and exeunt, separately.*)

QUEEN YU. Come, Great King: luckily the terrain around us here at Borderfoot is all high ridges and steep cliffs, not easy to attack or penetrate. Bide your time, await your chance, then scheme a way to break through the encirclement and seek aid. There will still be time!
XIANG YU. Ah me!
QUEEN YU. (*Forcing a smile*) Oh, I have made ready some wine. Let me drink a few more cups with you, Great King.
XIANG YU. Very well, then, bring me wine!
QUEEN YU. Come then, please, Great King.

(*Amid pipes and percussion they seat themselves.*)

QUEEN YU. Drink, Great King, I beg you.

(*They drink wine together.*)

XIANG YU. (*Throwing away his goblet*) Oh, oh, to think of it, Xiang Yu!
(*Sings*) I've the strength to uproot mountains, oh, I o'ershade
    the world in bravery,
  but times now run awry, oh, and Dapple can't gallop me
    free;
  Dapple can't gallop me free, oh, alas, alas, what is left for
    me?
  Oh my Yu, my Yu, what can I do, oh, there is no hope now
    left for me!

QUEEN YU. Hearing you sing with such full grief and bitter lamentation, Great King, makes one weep. So let me sing and dance for you to soothe your cares a while. May I?

XIANG YU. Aye ... ! It would be most kind of you, my royal Lady!

QUEEN YU. Very well then, I shall parade my pitiful skills.

(*Xiang Yu stares fixedly at Queen Yu. Queen Yu forces herself to be calm and, avoiding Xiang Yu's eyes, takes two swords and begins her dance.*)

QUEEN YU. (*Sings*)
  Drink, my sovereign lord, I pray, drink and listen to my lay,
  I shall melt your cares away by dancing light and whirling
    gay.
  Wicked Qin, the House of Ying, conquered all the land,
    world-wide held sway,
  till mighty heroes bold, on every hand, rose to fight in fierce
    array.
  They always said and always say: 'Abuse me not, nor treat me
    ill today,
  for failure and success are not to stay, but come and in a
    moment pass away.'
  So come, relax, give pleasure play, sit in your tent, all care
    with wine allay.

(*Queen Yu performs flourishes with the swords.*)

XIANG YU. (*Laughing bitterly*) A ha ha ....

(*Enter two grand eunuchs, together.*)

TWO GRAND EUNUCHS. We beg to inform you, Great King, that the enemy forces are coming to attack us from every side.

XIANG YU. Instruct my generals to divide into separate armies to meet the enemy on each front. There must be no delay in doing so!

TWO GRAND EUNUCHS. We obey your command (*Exeunt both, together.*)

XIANG YU. Oh, my royal Lady! The enemy are attacking us from all sides. Quickly! Quickly come with me, and we shall fight our way out through the dense encirclements.

QUEEN YU. Ah me! Oh, Great King! I could never make myself such a burden to you. Go forth now and do battle, and if things do not go well for you this time, retreat south of the Yangtse, and plan further moves from there. It is my prayer that I may have that sword at your waist, Great King, and cut my throat with it here in your presence, so that you will not be hampered by any more anxious longings for me.

XIANG YU. I ... I .... My royal Lady, you ... you must not put an end to your life.

QUEEN YU. Oh dear me, oh Great King. (*Sings*)
> The men of Han have seized our land,
> and all around sound songs of Chu.
> My lord, your spirit now is spent,
> and how could I live without you?

XIANG YU. Oh, woe is me! ...

(*Shouts backstage. Queen Yu starts with alarm. She demands Xiang Yu's sword from him. He refuses to give it to her.*)

XIANG YU. No, you can't do that, that's no good. You mustn't put an end to your life!

QUEEN YU. (*Using cunning*) Great King, Hạn soldiers ... they ... they're fighting their way in, they're coming towards us!

XIANG YU. Where? Let me see.

QUEEN YU. (*Seizes the opportunity to snatch the sword that Xiang Yu wears at his waist*) There! (*Cuts her own throat, and dies.*)

(*Enter four royal guards, unobtrusively.*)

XIANG YU. Woe is me! – Fetch my horse!

(*Exeunt four royal guards and Xiang Yu, together.*)

Scene Nine

(*Enter eight Han generals. They cross stage, then exeunt.*)

XIANG YU. (*Backstage, sings*)
> For several days I have toiled in battle, and hunger hard to
>   bear brings torture.

(Enter Xiang Yu. Enter one Han general in pursuit. He is stabbed to death by one thrust from Xiang Yu's spear.)

XIANG YU. *(Sings)*
> And Raven Dapple's lips are parched, unmoistened by fresh
> grass or water.

Hold hard. What have we now? Behind are the enemy soldiers pursuing me, and there before me lies the Great Yangtse. What on earth am I to do now!

MIN ZIQI. *(Backstage)* Cast loose, and we're under way!

(Enter Min Ziqi disguised as a fisherman, sculling his boat.)

MIN ZIQI. *(Sings)*
> I was given my orders in the Field Marshal's headquarters,
> and go wait in ambush down by the Yangtse waters.

Reverent greetings to you, Great King. The soldiers pursuing you are already here. Swiftly, swiftly, board my boat.

XIANG YU. I have been utterly routed: how could I have the face to meet the elders of the land south of the Yangtse? Take my warhorse across the Yangtse, and set him free there.

(Xiang Yu lets go his horse. Min Ziqi takes the horse, but it jumps into the Yangtse. Exit Min Ziqi, unobtrusively.)

XIANG YU. Ah me ...! *(Sings)*
> Though a horse, he could love his master, his nature was
> ardent fidelity.
> How he shames the turncoat wretch, who quits his lord
> perfidiously.

(Enter Lü Matong.)

LÜ MATONG. Reverent greetings, Great King.

XIANG YU. You have come just at the right moment, General Lü. Liu Bang has previously promised that anyone who obtains my head will be given a reward of a thousand pieces of gold. I am now going to cut off my head, so you, general, may go and collect the reward for that noble deed.

LÜ MATONG. You do me too much honour, insignificant officer that I am.

XIANG YU. Oh woe is me, general! *(Sings)*
> My picked Army of Eight Thousand Youths is all dispersed,
> though there be a ferry across the Raven River, I will not go.
> How could I face the elders south of the Yangtse?

(Says) Enough! *(Sings)*
> Best to put paid to this remnant life with one swift blow! *(Cuts
his own throat, and dies.)*

(*Enter all Han generals and Liu Bang, together.*)

LÜ MATONG. Xiang Yu is dead.
LIU BANG. Cease the war!

(*Exeunt all, together.*)

Identifying footprints in the snow

Chuanju drama: version (anon.) of the mid-1950s

Characters:

LI KINGFISHER SCREEN: young lady, daughter of a prime minister.
LÜ MENGZHENG: young scholar, husband of Li Kingfisher Screen.

(*Enter Kingfisher Screen.*)

KINGFISHER SCREEN.
 (*Sings*) Serene is my heart and firm is my will.

(*Where she enters, she chops some wood and cooks some rice. Crosses stage.*)

 Mengzheng my husband's just a student, we're helplessly
  poor,
 his genius of no avail, he's at the temple seeking charity fare;
 but I fear in this whirling snowstorm he'll get frozen to the
  core;
 I sit forlorn in the cold kiln, eager to see him back once more.

(*Falls asleep. Enter Mengzheng.*)

MENGZHENG. (*Sings*)
 I return to the kiln through the snow, feeling sodden from
  head to toe,
 to the kiln where my wife must undergo sorrows sore and
  heavy woe;·
 So I hasten my steps, press onward, and, glancing round as I
  go, (*looks at ground*)
 I see footprints of a man and woman, intertwining to and fro.

(*Looks again.*)

 But who'd come visiting this lonely village, though?
 – There's something very odd about these footprints in the
  snow.
(*Says*) Now why would there be the footprints of a man and woman
outside the door of the kiln? (*Thinks*) Ah, her parents, seeing that
the weather's so cold, must have sent a man to take her back to
their residence. Oh, wife, wife, if you wanted to go back home, you
at least might have waited till I got back before you left. (*Thinks*)
No, no, that can't be it. After all, it was because my wife refused to
obey her father's orders that she was driven out of his prime-

ministerial residence in the first place. So her parents wouldn't be sending anyone to take her back there, would they? (*Thinks*) You know, her being a girl from a mandarin's family, she must find all this poverty and hardship unbearable, mustn't she? These footprints, a man's and a woman's ... surely she can't have ... a new lover? But she's always been so good and faithful – she'd never do such a thing. Oh dear, though, you can't tell for certain. These last few days I've drawn a blank in my efforts to get free food from the monastery, and the other day she even had a quarrel with me. So you never know, she ... But let's go in and see. (*Crosses stage. Sings*)

I hurry to the kiln once more.

(*Enters kiln.*)

(*Says*) Hey! Fancy that though, she's gone to sleep!
(*Sings*)
I see my pretty wife in heavy slumber,
thought to call her, but I'll wait till she wakes and discuss
things at leisure.
In the early days my poverty never earned me her displeasure,
but yes, since we came to this cold kiln together,
we've lived from hand to mouth and ill-clad for bitter
weather.
(*Says*) Wife, oh my wife, my poverty is but the poverty of the winter. Just wait till next spring. (*Sings*)
When my hour comes, the dragon of success I'll bridle and
tether.
(*Says*) Oh yes, just wait till next spring. My luck'll turn. My hour will come. Don't worry – I'll soar to eminence, I'll ride to high office. (*Shows that he is feeling cold.*) Oh heaven on high, send wind or snow if you must, but why not send them singly? (*Shows that he is feeling cold.*) I never managed to get any charity food at the temple, only a full course of mockery. And that driving snowstorm's soaked me. I picked up some reeds and brushwood on the way, so I might as well burn some firewood and dry my clothes while I'm waiting, and when that hussy wakes up, I'll have it out with her. (*Looks round.*) Now why to goodness is there nothing to get a light from in this kiln? Can't even find any matches. (*Searches*) Ah, here are some. (*Lights a fire in the fireplace, crumples some paper and, as he blows a flame up, says*) It's bad enough if a good man's not yet made his mark in the world, but then he has to go and suffer abuse from nobodies into the bargain. When I fulfill my ambitions, those two scurvy baldies, those monks Tang Seven and Tang Eight, will learn what a terror His Worship Lü Mengzheng can be! (*Makes grim*

expressions. Blows fire out.) Aw, it's not only nobodies who treat you badly – even the fire goes out on you when you're trying to blow it alight! Right, have it your own way, I just won't dry myself then! (*Throws firewood on the floor, where it forms the shape of the Chinese word for 'ten'.*) Hey now, that firewood has fallen on the floor in the pattern of the word 'ten'. An inspiration for my poetic muse! I'll compose a poem on the topic of the word 'ten'. Yes, ten – (*Thinks*) 'Ten times I sought a charity meal and nine times failed.' Hm, if I open with seeking charity meals, I'll have to end on that note: don't tell me His Worship Lü Mengzheng is going to be completely dependent on the Maudgalyāyana Monastery for his survival! (*Thinks again*) Aha,

> Ten ... ten times you knock, nine it stays closed, the wealthy man's door.
> My head covered in snow, I turn back home once more;
> empty-handed, I can't help us against hunger and freezing cold,
> we face each other sad of mien, our's a lot indeed to deplore.

Oh, no, that 'deplore''s no good. 'Endure' –

> we face each other sad of mien, our lot hard to endure.

(*Thinks*) Yes, that's the same general category of rhyme ... 'deplore', 'endure'. (*Makes gestures betraying his hunger*) Oh dear me, my tummy's rumbling, I'm so hungry. This hunger and freezing cold's unbearable, and I suppose I'll have to put up with that, too, in a bit? (*Sings*)

> This hunger and this cold there's no prospect of relieving,
> How can I tell her? What can I say?
> My tummy is rumbling, my heart is all trembling,

(*Shivers.*)

> and the wild wind and snowstorm like arrows are piercing.
> Ten times you knock, nine it stays shut, the wealthy man's door,
> I've battled through the snowstorm back home here once more,
> fireless and riceless, we can't get warm or still our hunger,
> she'll grumble and she'll ask 'What's all your learning good for?'
> Worse still, I'm afraid I'll lose my wife, she won't stay.

KINGFISHER SCREEN. (*Waking up. Sings*)

> What do you mean: your wife cannot stay?
> She can bear up against hunger and the chill winter day.
> I can see my man, home from the snow, thin coat all wet, so without delay,
> I quickly undo my silk skirt from my waist,
> and give it to my husband to keep the cold air away.

(*She puts her silk skirt over the top of Mengzheng to protect him.*)

MENGZHENG. Now why do I suddenly feel much warmer? (*Takes off silk skirt and looks at it in astonishment.*) Well, I ask you, what on earth is this?

KINGFISHER SCREEN. It's my silk skirt.

MENGZHENG. Silk skirts are things you wear round your bottom half, so what do you mean by putting it over my head? Really, you're insulting my scholarly dignity. (*Throws skirt to floor.*)

KINGFISHER SCREEN. Aren't you cold, then?

MENGZHENG. A man worth his salt is not chilled even by cold weather. Look, I'm not even shivering. (*Shivers.*)

KINGFISHER SCREEN. (*Sings*)
>Oh husband,
>in such bitter mid-winter weather as today,
>keep out the cold, if you may, whatever the way.

MENGZHENG. A disciple of our Sage, Confucius, makes not the slightest move without correct decorum. How can you put a silk skirt over a scholar?

KINGFISHER SCREEN. (*Sings*)
>My husband, I cannot persuade you by what I say;
>let me bring you some rice-pudding your hunger to allay.

(*Serves rice-pudding to Mengzheng. At the sight of it, he stares fixedly at Kingfisher Screen for a while, his facial expression indicating that his thoughts are travelling from food to footprints.*)

MENGZHENG. It stinks unbearably.

KINGFISHER SCREEN. It stinks? What do you mean?

MENGZHENG. It's unclean.

KINGFISHER SCREEN. White rice boiled in water – how can you say it's unclean?

MENGZHENG. I'm not sticking that. Quickly, away!

KINGFISHER SCREEN. You want a little less to eat?

MEGZHENG. I would prefer to be pure and poor than rich and filthy.

KINGFISHER SCREEN. What on earth are you on about? All right, don't eat it then.

MENGZHENG. Right, and now can you clarify one or two things for me? Might I ask you what that is in front of us there?

KINGFISHER SCREEN. A narrow, dangerous, winding track.

MENGZHENG. And there behind us?

KINGFISHER SCREEN. A forest that only rooks can pass through.

MENGZHENG. Ah, so you've found that out, too, have you? (*Sings*)
>Since there's a perilous track to the front and impassable
>   wood to the rear,
>in this bleak deserted village that few if any ever walk near,

and since we'd used all the rice and firewood we had here,
from where did this bowl of rice-pudding suddenly appear?

KINGFISHER SCREEN. Oh, you're wondering about this rice-pudding, is that it? There's a story behind how that got here.

MENGZHENG. Yes, a story behind how that got here! What way it came ... Fat lot of good your being a prime minister's daughter – you've no notion of morality, no comprehension of the scriptures. Oh, you! (*Sings*)

What's the good your being the posh daughter of a premier?
you lack all sense of modesty, decorum, moral honour.
Compared with loss of chastity, the truly good think nought
of death from hunger,
You've cast our pillow-and-quilt love-whispers away down
the vast rolling sewer!

KINGFISHER SCREEN. (*Aside*) My scholar has come back looking disgruntled and he's talking wildly. Must be some bothersome inner dilemma irritating him. You know, we've never had any trouble of this sort since we've been married. But I'd better ask him a few questions and try and clear the matter up. (*To Mengzheng*) Scholar, you haven't asked me a thing since you came back, so how do you know so much?

MENGZHENG. (*Sings*)

Oh no, I'm not asking what's happened,
but you know very well what I mean, all about the matter!

KINGFISHER SCREEN. Scholar, you've been out all day, and now you've come home you're sneering at me and making scathing insinuations. Don't you have any thought for how your wife suffers cold and hunger, and all for you?

MENGZHENG. Well, you need rice and firewood to stop you being cold and hungry.

KINGFISHER SCREEN. Well, bring some.

MENGZHENG. Eh, what?

KINGFISHER SCREEN. Firewood and rice.

MENGZHENG. (*Aside*) The hussy's demanding firewood and rice from me! Right, I must trick her outdoors and make her confess to me whose the footprints are. (*To Kingfisher Screen*) The firewood and rice are outside under the window.

KINGFISHER SCREEN. Then why don't you bring them into the kiln?

MENGZHENG. I can't carry them.

KINGFISHER SCREEN. I'll lend you a hand. (*They go out of the kiln together.*) Where are the firewood and rice? Eh, scholar? The firewood and the rice?

MENGZHENG. Ah, firewood and rice ... we're the only 'firewood

142

and rice' – those two mutually indispensable things, husband and wife.

KINGFISHER SCREEN. Since there's no firewood or rice, what have you tricked me out here for? (*Is about to enter the kiln.*)

MENGZHENG. (*Barring her way*) It's so boring just sitting doing nothing in the kiln. I tricked you out here to look at the scenery.

KINGFISHER SCREEN. In the kind of predicament we're in, scholar, how can we feel like looking at scenery?

MENGZHENG. By looking at scenery one can ward off cold and by examining the snow one can ascertain betrayal.

KINGFISHER SCREEN. What rubbish are you talking?

MENGZHENG. Look how pretty the path is, wife!

KINGFISHER SCREEN. But scholar, the pretty scenery's up there on the hills.

MENGZHENG. No, look down there on the ground, wife – there's some really pretty scenery now!

KINGFISHER SCREEN. Oh no, scholar, the really pretty scenery's up there, against the sky.

MENGZHENG. (*In a fury*) Huh, when I say the path, you say the hills, and when I say the ground, you say the sky. Now that really makes me rather suspicious.

KINGFISHER SCREEN. Suspicious about what, scholar?

MENGZHENG. Tell me, what's that up there?

KINGFISHER SCREEN. Ice on the trees.

MENGZHENG. And what's that down there?

KINGFISHER SCREEN. That's snow, on grass.

MENGZHENG. And what's on top of it?

KINGFISHER SCREEN. Loose snowflakes.

MENGZHENG. And what's next to the loose snowflakes?

KINGFISHER SCREEN. Withered plants.

MENGZHENG. No, this is what I mean.

KINGFISHER SCREEN. What?

MENGZHENG. These!

KINGFISHER SCREEN. Eh? What?

MENGZHENG. (*Impatiently pulling Kingfisher Screen's foot aside*)This, this, this!

KINGFISHER SCREEN. Oh, that? (*Puckering her lips in a suppressed smile. Aside*) Why I do believe that my scholar's arrived back in the kiln in such a bad temper today all because he's seen some footprints and it's made him suspicious. (*Thinks*) Well, I won't give him any explanations just yet. I'll tease my little scholar a bit! (*To Mengzheng*) You mean these footprints, the man's and the woman's?

MENGZHENG. Yes, whose are the man's footprints?

KINGFISHER SCREEN. They're ... yours!

MENGZHENG. I'm wearing straw shoes. These are footprints from boots with nails in the soles.

KINGFISHER SCREEN. Well, surely you've heard the saying, my scholar, that 'When bold ambition one's bosom fills, one's straw shoes change to fine boots with nails'!

MENGZHENG. Oh, so, 'When bold ambition one's bosom fills, one's straw shoes change to fine boots with nails'? All right, and what about these small ones?

KINGFISHER SCREEN. The small ones ... they're yours, too.

MENGZHENG. Well, that certainly is magic! All right, I know: 'When one day with ill-luck you meet, your big feet shrink to little feet'!

KINGFISHER SCREEN. (*Laughs*) They're your wife's footprints, scholar.

MENGZHENG. So you didn't stay in the kiln? What brought you outside?

KINGFISHER SCREEN. I came out to watch for you!

MENGZHENG. To watch for me, eh?

KINGFISHER SCREEN. Yes, to watch for you!

MENGZHENG. If you'd come to watch for me, they'd only be just in front of the kiln, or just behind, or just at the sides. How is it you went watching for me right along that dangerous winding track?

KINGFISHER SCREEN. I just kept on taking steps forward as I watched for you, and I ended up looking for you along that winding track.

MENGZHENG. (*Disbelieving. Speaking sardonically*) So kind of you, I'm sure. So very kind!

KINGFISHER SCREEN. (*With seemly modesty*) Not at all! Your gratitude shames me.

MENGZHENG. (*Sardonically*) My gratitude shames you. – There are three great things in life that not to live up to really is a matter of shame!

KINGFISHER SCREEN. What three things?

MENGZHENG. By wealth and splendour one must not be dazzled. Before might and power one must not bend. By poverty and lowly condition one must not be swerved.

KINGFISHER SCREEN. Well, I wouldn't dare make any rash claims about anyone else, but, as far as I myself am concerned, *I* can live up to those things.

MENGZHENG. Oh no you couldn't, not you!

KINGFISHER SCREEN. Yes, me. I can. Remember how in the old days when I was up there in my Many-coloured Wedding Bower and had to select myself a husband by throwing the silk whip down at him? There were any number of princes, noblemen and successful graduate literati there, but it was none of them I hit. I saw then that you were more of a fine genius than any of them, and you and none other were the one on whom I bestowed the silk whip. Doesn't that count as not being dazzled by wealth and splendour?

MENGZHENG. All right, yes, it does.

KINGFISHER SCREEN. Then when you and I, as husband and wife, went into the prime minister's residence together to submit the news to my father, the prime minister, he, seeing that you were so poor, wanted me to back out of the marriage agreement, and it was because I swore I'd rather die than obey him that we were both driven out by my father ... the prime minister. Now, might that not count as not bending before might and power?

MENGZHENG. All right, yes, it does. But one thing I'm afraid you can't live up to is not being swerved by your poverty and lowly condition.

KINGFISHER SCREEN. Oh, I can manage that even better. I've come with you into this cold kiln, living from hand to mouth, with inadequate clothing, and I've contentedly borne poverty as if it had always been my condition, without the slightest grumble. Now haven't I achieved perfection in that respect?

MENGZHENG. (At a loss for words) Er – ?

KINGFISHER SCREEN. In fact, why say perfection? More than perfection!

MENGZHENG. But even if a stone is made of precious green jade, if it's got a flaw in it, do you think that you can still call it 'more than perfect'?

KINGFISHER SCREEN. Troubles start with suspicions. It's you who are so concerned with station in life and reputation, you poor –

MENGZHENG. Poor fool?

KINGFISHER SCREEN. Oh scholar, you said it, scholar!

MENGZHENG. Huh, you think I'm poor today, but how do you know I won't be rich some day? And if one day I hit the heights and become world-famous, I'm going to thoroughly humiliate that prime minister father of yours, and I'll subject your mother to shame, and I'll make you feel small, too, you precious young milady!

KINGFISHER SCREEN. Scholar, if you hit the heights, my suffering all this hunger and cold and all my hardships and toil will not have been in vain.

MENGZHENG. I, Mengzheng, regard the attainment of fame and success as mere 'grass and cress', as Mencius says, but then ... I'm afraid you're not cut out to be a noble lady!

KINGFISHER SCREEN. I'm afraid you're not cut out for the heights, though of course I'll be all right as a noble lady.

MENGZHENG. (*Mockingly*) So, I have before me a lady of nobility, then!

KINGFISHER SCREEN. That's right.

MENGZHENG. After you then, my lady. (*Ushers her as if into a palace.*)

KINGFISHER SCREEN. Thank you. (*Is about to enter the kiln.*)

MENGZHENG. Not so fast. We haven't cleared up the footprints yet.

(*Bars her way.*)

KINGFISHER SCREEN. When the sun comes out they'll clear up by themselves.

MENGZHENG. No, that won't clear them up.

KINGFISHER SCREEN. Sweep them.

MENGZHENG. Oh, no, you can't brush them off.

KINGFISHER SCREEN. Well, wash them away.

MENGZHENG. No, that won't remove the dirt.

KINGFISHER SCREEN. All right, just leave them be!

MENGZHENG. Leave them be? You may want to leave them be, but I'm not going to. Just tell me: can you identify those footprints? If so, then come in and see me in the kiln. If you can't identify them, then rather die than look upon my face again. Huh, no morals whatsoever! (*Enters kiln.*)

KINGFISHER SCREEN. (*Seeing him go into the kiln, laughs*) I mustn't tease the priggish scholar to death! I'd better go in and explain things to him.

MENGZHENG. (*Coming out at the same time as Kingfisher Screen goes in*) Hm, she sounds as if she's talking with somebody. I'll go out and have a look. (*The two of them bang heads in the doorway of the kiln.*)

MENGZHENG. Hey, who's that?

KINGFISHER SCREEN. Are you hitting me?

MENGZHENG. That's it. Let's go in and do some hitting.

(*Kingfisher Screen goes into the kiln. Mengzheng picks up a stick and strikes out at her. She at once lifts up a cooking-pot to ward off the blow.*)

MENGZHENG. (*Flabbergasted*) When a married couple are having a fight cooking-pots shouldn't come between them. Put it down.

KINGFISHER SCREEN. You put that down. (*They simultaneously put the things down.*) Who do you think you're hitting?

MENGZHENG. Somebody wearing nailed boots.

KINGFISHER SCREEN. Oh deary dear, my dear husband! (*Sings*)

I urge you, husband mine, to entertain no wild suspicion.

MENGZHING. The proof is there, we've got the evidence. Is that entertaining wild suspicions?

KINGFISHER SCREEN. (*Sings*)

Listen now to my clarification:
(But look at his face, see his expression,
– you can tell he's too angry to hear explanation!
Just because of rice-pud and his mystification
he's whipped up this trouble and tribulation!)
Oh deary me, my scholar husband,
and you a studious man, packed with Confucian education,
so punctilious about integrity and moral elevation!

MENGZHENG. All this time you've been talking, those are the first nice words I've heard from you.

KINGFISHER SCREEN. But what has your wife said that wasn't nice?

MENGZHENG. Don't try and praise yourself up with me! You haven't been speaking nicely at all! I don't want to hear!

KINGFISHER SCREEN. (*Aside*) I thought I'd explain things to him, but he's still so vicious and stubborn I'll tease him a bit more. Stand aside, scholar, I'm going out.

MENGZHENG. I won't allow you to go out.

KINGFISHER SCREEN. You can't stop me.

MENGZHENG. What, so I can't even stop her now? (*Kingfisher Screen goes out of the kiln. Mengzheng picks up the stick and goes out after her.*)

KINGFISHER SCREEN. (*Deliberately talking to herself*) The next time you come, don't wear nailed boots. Wear straw shoes, so that my scholar doesn't have to examine the footprints and get all puzzled and confused!

MENGZHENG. Oh, oh, you're exasperating me to death! (*Grasps stick and makes as if to cut his own throat with it. At the sight of him doing so, Kingfisher Screen bursts out laughing. Mengzheng puts down the stick and clouts himself round the head with his hand. The two of them enter the kiln together.*)

KINGFISHER SCREEN. Oh, scholar! (*Sings*)
The more I try to explain,
the more and more puzzled he gets again;
I'm teasing him mad, I'd better refrain
and tell him from where those footprints came!
My mother, doting on her daughter (unbeknown, though, to
    my father)
sent the old butler with rice and silver, money and grain,
our lot to sustain.
But you came back to the kiln and gave me no chance to
    explain,
instead uttered words that caused me much pain.
In view of that, I would maintain
that it's you in the wrong and it's me should complain.
(*Says*) When you got back here, scholar, you never asked the ins and

outs, just conceived a lot of wild suspicions, opening the floodgates of random accusations. Dear me now, I don't think that's how a scholar should behave, is it?

MENGZHENG. (*Aside*) Come to think of it, my wife's never had enough clothes to keep herself warm since she came to this kiln, nor enough food to satisfy her hunger, but she's never voiced the slightest grumble. She could never have done what I thought, could she? And what's more, if her mother's sent a man over to bring some silver and rice, it'll mean a few days less hunger and cold for me, too. Yes, I really have been a fine generous soul with a mean man's niggardly outlook. This mustn't go on any longer. Mm, yes, oh dear yes, I really must stop it at once ... Ah, yes, as my wife's so gentle and mild and noble-minded, all I need do is go up to her and bow my apologies, and everything's sure to be all right again. (*To Kingfisher Screen*) I'm a worthless fellow. I've offended you by my words. But you're so tolerant and understanding, dear wife, and if I speak frankly I'm sure you won't lose your temper with me. I bow to you in apology, my wife. (*Bows*)

KINGFISHER SCREEN. Scholar! Such things cannot be treated as a child's game.

MENGZHENG. Oh no, oh no, of course not, it's no small matter, to be sure. Of course, I can't hope to settle things just by a bow. I must make full apology. See, wife, see what I'm doing before you now. (*Kneels.*)

KINGFISHER SCREEN. Well, scholar, in everything one does one must first think, think and think again. Next time it will be no good. Now quickly, quickly, I bid you rise!

MENGZHENG. Thank you, you're very kind. (*Stands up*) Wife, what do you mean? – Did your mother send the old butler here with rice and silver, then?

KINGFISHER SCREEN. Yes, the butler's just left, a little while ago.

MENGZHENG. Where have you put the silver?

KINGFISHER SCREEN. I put it in that waterlogged boot you picked up the other day.

MENGZHENG. (*Hastily covering up her mouth*) Leather casket. Just say you put the silver in the leather casket. Put the silver in the leather casket. (*Aside*) I've offended my wife today, so I'll have to try and coax a merry laugh from her. (*Takes out silver and says to the silver*) I feel rather resentful towards you.

KINGFISHER SCREEN. What do you feel resentful towards it for?

MENGZHENG. I recall that when His Worship Lü Mengzheng's parents were alive, (*points at silver*) you were a constant caller. But once they'd left this world, you hopped it. Most offensive thing to do. Well, today we meet again, and don't imagine I can show you any mercy. You there! Haul him down and flog him!

KINGFISHER SCREEN. Oh scholar, what on earth are you doing? Are you going soft in the head now?

MENGZHENG. Very well, in view of the fact that my wife has spoken on your behalf, I shall on this occasion spare you punishment. Therefore, now bow your head in thanks to my good lady. (*The two of them laugh together. He puts the silver down.*) What about the rice, then, wife?

KINGFISHER SCREEN. The rice is in the waste-paper basket.

MENGZHENG. (*Hastily stopping her*) Oh, so the rice is in the rice-garner.

KINGFISHER SCREEN. Oh, yes, yes. In the rice-garner.

MENGZHENG. (*Taking out some rice and looking at it.*) Good rice, that, good rice. (*One grain of rice drops onto the floor. He goes to pick it up.*)

KINGFISHER SCREEN. Scholar, one grain of rice won't make a rice-broth. Don't bother picking it up.

MENGZHENG. Come, come, wife, that won't do, that won't do. A man in olden times spoke well when he said:

Weeding the grain in the midday sun,
into the soil the sweatdrops run;
to think that the food in our dish
is every grain by hard toil won!

KINGFISHER SCREEN. Yes, that's so right, you know.

MENGZHENG. (*Putting down the rice*)
Now let's not pick at each other, let's let the matter lie.

KINGFISHER SCREEN.
But the rights and wrongs must be decided!

MENGZHENG.
The clouds and mists have cleared from our sky.

KINGFISHER SCREEN.
As a pair, our balance is somewhat lobsided.

MENGZHENG. I think we're a perfect married couple.

KINGFISHER SCREEN. Between a perfect married couple there can be no doubting this and suspecting that!

MENGZHENG. (*Giving her a winning smile*) Wife, now, nobody except a saint's without faults, are they? And there's no greater virtue than to mend one's ways when one's gone wrong. (*Indicates that he is hungry*) Wife, quickly now, serve me up a bowl of rice-pudding!

KINGFISHER SCREEN. But it's cold now, I'm afraid, scholar.

MENGZHENG. Never mind. Cold tea and cold rice don't bother me.

KINGFISHER SCREEN. But cold words and insinuations do bother one. They're very hurtful.

MENGZHENG. Wife, you – you're bringing it up again!

KINGFISHER SCREEN. (*Looks at the cooking pot*) Well, scholar, the rice on top is cold, but underneath's still hot. I'll bring you some. (*Dishes out rice-pudding and gives it to Mengzheng. Mengzheng takes the bowl and is about to eat.*) Wait a moment, I've got a few questions I want to ask you first.

MENGZHENG. Ask me when I've eaten.

KINGFISHER SCREEN. No, hang on. Just now when you came back to the kiln looking so terribly cold and hungry and I served you a bowl of rice-pudding, you said something to me. Do you remember what you said?

MENGZHENG. It was just foolish nonsense. Let's talk about that when I've eaten.

KINGFISHER SCREEN. No, wait a moment. You said it stank unbearably. What did you mean by that?

MENGZHENG. Well, I, er ...

KINGFISHER SCREEN. Isn't that what you said?

MENGZHENG. Yes, that's right. But you must have misconstrued. When I went to the temple to try and get some food today there was a gale and a snowstorm and a thick mist everywhere, and I was just remarking that the mist was unbearable. There's no trace of unpleasant smell about such excellent rice-pudding, is there, now?

KINGFISHER SCREEN. Oh, so it was the mist that was unbearable?

MENGZHENG. Mm. (*Is again about to eat.*)

KINGFISHER SCREEN. Just a minute. You also said something about 'unclean'. Who isn't clean?

MENGZHENG. Er, er well ... yes, I did say that, too. Well, when I went to try and get the food from the temple today, the path was so slippery I tripped and fell flat and got covered all over in mud. As you were serving me the rice-pudding, I noticed my hands weren't clean. I would never have said that you were unclean! (*Makes to eat again.*)

KINGFISHER SCREEN. There was something else: you said something about not sticking it and taking it away. What did you mean?

MENGZHENG. Ah yes, quite right. Well, wife, I noticed that you had cooked a nice thin rice-pudding, and as I was hungry and impatient to eat, I thought I'd dispense with chopsticks and just pick it up and drink it straight down, the quickest and easiest way. Like that I thought I wouldn't need the sticks and you could take them away.

KINGFISHER SCREEN. It doesn't matter you saying those things, but something else you said really did upset me very much.

MENGZHENG. Oh, what was that?

KINGFISHER SCREEN. You said you'd prefer to be pure and poor than rich and filthy.

MENGZHENG. Well, er ...

KINGFISHER SCREEN. Tell me, who is it that's pure and poor, and who is it that's rich and filthy?

MENGZHENG. You must have misheard me, wife! I could see you were in such a nervy state as you served me the rice-pudding, and I was afraid you might break the cooking-pot. So I was just telling you to be pure, er *sure* and *pour* carefully from the pot and not *pitch* a *healthy* vessel and break it. A way of urging that such a well-tried and worthy servant should not meet with destruction. Oh no, a disciple of Confucius our Sage never utters unseemly words, so I'd certainly not have said 'pure and poor' and 'rich and filthy' or whatever it was, would I now?

KINGFISHER SCREEN. Oh, scholar, now let me ask you: When you went to the temple to try and get some food today, what sort of treatment did you receive from Tang Seven and Tang Eight?

MENGZHENG. The very mention of Tang Seven and Tang Eight makes my blood boil. In the past it's always been the custom to ring the dinner-bell before the meal. But today they ate the food first before they rang the dinner-bell. So by the time I got there, there was nothing to be had. Tang Seven and Tang Eight were warming themselves, hogging all the fire, and when I appeared they completely ignored me. I was terribly hungry and cold, so I thought of a trick. I tore a piece off my blue shirt and lobbed the piece into the fire. As the two of them smelled the smell of burning cloth, they started saying 'My son, your coat's on fire!' and 'Father, your coat's on fire!', and no sooner had the pair of them leapt up than I took my seat by the fire, able to enjoy it all to myself. Don't you think that was a good trick, eh, wife?

KINGFISHER SCREEN. (*With irony*) Only Scholar Lü Mengzheng could think up such a trick.

MENGZHENG. Hm, but their tricks went one better than mine. Tang Seven said, 'My son, look, His Worship Lü has been here all this time – why don't you serve him some tea?'

KINGFISHER SCREEN. So they did show you some respect then?

MENGZHENG. Wife! That Tang Eight came up with a huge cup of tea, and, with faultless timing, at the very moment he reached the fire he upset the cup, and kerash splash – (*Knocks his own bowl of rice-pudding over. The rice-pudding falls to the floor.*)

KINGFISHER SCREEN. It's spilt, scholar!

MENGZHENG. Yes, spilt, the lot.

KINGFISHER SCREEN. Yours, scholar, it's spilt!

MENGZHENG. Well, it put the whole fire out! – Not half it spilt!

KINGFISHER SCREEN. No, scholar, *you* have spilt your rice-pudding.

MENGZHENG. (*Looks in dismay*) Ow! (*Sings*)

Oh how wretched it makes me feel!

My misery's more than I can tell!
All the hunger I've borne, and the cold as well,
now my rice-pud's spilt and I've lost my meal!
(*Says*) Oh dear, all my rice-pudding's spilt on the floor.
KINGFISHER SCREEN. Oh, scholar, don't get upset now. The rice-pudding's spilt, but there's still some rice. Come with me and I'll boil you some plain dry rice.
MENGZHENG. Some plain dry rice, eh? Come on, let's go!

(*Exeunt together.*)

Notes

Introduction

1. Arthur H. Smith, *Chinese Characteristics*, New York, Chicago and Toronto, Fleming H. Revell Company, 1897, 3rd ed., ch.1, pp.16–17. My attention was drawn to these points by an article of Luo Jintang's: 'Zhongguorende xijuguan', *Mingbao* monthly, Hong Kong, Jan. 1973, pp.30–5.
2. This question is discussed in some detail in William Dolby, *A History of Chinese Drama*, London, Paul Elek, 1976.
3. Translated from *Yuanqu xuan waibian*, 2 vols, ed. Sui Shusen, Peking Zhonghua Shuju, 1959, vol.1, pp.428–31.
4. Translated from *Yongle dadian* (1403–4), compiled by Xie Jin (1369–1415) and others, remnant volumes, Peking, Zhonghua Shuju, 1960, fo. 139991, pp.54b–60a.
5. Translated from *Yuanqu xuan* ('Selection of Yuan songs') (1615–6), compiled by Zang Maoxun (d.1621), 4 vols, Peking, Wenxue Guji, 1955, vol.2, pp.542–56.
6. Translated from *Liu-shi-zhong qu*, ed. Mao Jin (1598–1659), Shanghai, Wenxue Guji, 1955, pt 3, pp.17–21.
7. Translated from Zhou Yibai (ed.), *Mingren zaju xuan*, Peking, Renmin Wenxue, 1958, pp.261–68.
8. Translated from *Zhui bai-qiu* (1770), compiled by Wanhuazhuren (mid-eighteenth century) and Qian Decang, Taipei, Zhong Hua Shuju, 1967, pt 6, pp.23–9.
9. Translated from *Mei Lanfang yanchu juben xuanji*, Hong Kong, Shijie Publishers, 1956, pp.121–55.
10. Guanzhong: a name for present-day Shensi province in the north-west of China, a key strategic area and excellent terrain for a military base.
11. King Huai of Chu, named Xin, a descendant of the pre-Qin kings of Chu. Xiang Yu's father set up Xin, a shepherd at the time, as King Huai. Xiang Yu later accorded him the title of Honorary Emperor, but then proceeded to divide up China between the various victors over Qin and later set himself up as Hegemon King of Chu with his capital at Pengcheng in Kiangsu, banishing the Honorary Emperor to the far south in 206 BC.
12. In Anhwei, where Xiang Yu died.

13. Translated from *Zhonghua huoye wenxuan*, 61–70, Zhonghua Shuju, 1962, pp.43–4.
14. Translated from *Renmin wenxue* (Peking), no.11, 1952, pp.49–53.

Grandee's son takes the wrong career

1. Datong in present-day Shantung province. It was the Western Capital of the Liao (947–1211) and Jin (1115–1234) dynasties.
2. i.e. the Hanlin Academy, an assembly of literary genius at the imperial court.
3. Liu Shiqing, otherwise known as Liu Yong, was an early eleventh-century poet of *ci* poetry. Both his poems and his personal life were renowned for their concern with romantic love.
4. The poet Du Fu (712–70), one of China's two most famous poets.
5. In Chinese, as in Indian and other mythologies, there is a rabbit on the moon.
6. The original says 'hump-backed turtle'. 'Turtle' was used as a slang term for 'cuckold' and also for the husband of a whore, i.e. one who was his wife's procurer.
7. Sima Rangju of the Spring and Autumn period (770–481 BC)?
8. Pang Juan was a general of the Kingdom of Wei during the mid-fourth century BC.
9. Or posters? Seemingly only naming the performer(s).
10. Entertainers were legally bound, when called upon, to provide entertainment for government officials and at official receptions. The penalties for failing to do so, or for inadequacies in the entertainment, were severe, and the task seems to have been feared.
11. Xiao He (d.193 BC) was a famous minister of the first emperor of the Han dynasty. The reference must be to some story about him.
12. Reference to some story or saying no longer known.
13. This seems to be a lewd pun in the Chinese, and probably echoes in its allusiveness, and thus seems to mock, the exchange between Shouma and Golden Notice.
14. There was a Sòng *guanben zaju* called *Wang Kui thrice takes the local examinations*, and during the years 1190–4 a *nanxi* play on Wang Kui enjoyed great popularity. There seem to have been various *nanxi* on the theme. A Yuan *zaju* by Shang Zhongxian (thirteenth-fourteenth century) was called *Wang Kui is faithless to Cassia Beauty*, and Yang Wenkui of the late fourteenth century

wrote a *zaju* called *Wang Kui is not faithless*. The Wang Kui story was very popular during the Sông and Yuan. It concerned the scholar Wang Kui who failed the examinations, but later, helped by the singing-girl Cassia Beauty, came out Top Graduate. Then, however, he broke his vows to her and took another wife.

15. A Yuan *zaju* by Zheng Tingyu (thirteenth-fourteenth century) and an anonymous Yuan or early Ming *nanxi* both had this title, and there is also a Jin or Yuan *yuanben* entitled *Meng Jiang Maiden*. The story tells how Meng went to the distant Great Wall to find her husband, who was working there, and found that he had been killed and interred in the Wall. She wept so bitterly that the Wall collapsed, revealing his bones.

16. There was a *nanxi* called *Xue Cloud Lady as a ghost plays matchmaker*. The story was probably that Cloud Lady, appearing (from out of a portrait?) as a spirit, managed to bring together her daughter and the son of someone to whom she owed a debt of gratitude.

17. The story may be that of Zhuo Refined Lady and her love-affair with the famous poet Sima Xiangru, on which theme there were a Sông *guanben zaju*; a *nanxi*; and several Yuan *zaju*, by Guan Hanqing (*c.* 1220–1300), Qu Gongying (fourteenth century), Fan Juzhong (thirteenth-fourteenth century) *et alia*; and other works. There was an anonymous Yuan *zaju* entitled *Love-birds' meeting*.

18. On the love affair of scholar Guo Hua and the rouge-seller Wang Moon Beauty. There was an anonymous Yuan *zaju* called *Leaving the slipper* on this theme, and the *yuanben Foolish Master Guo* may perhaps also have used the subject. I translate, later in this collection, the play *Buying rouge* which is a much later play on the same theme.

19. There is a Yuan *zaju* by Yang Xianzhi (thirteenth century) called *Riverside travel-halt and night rain by the River Xiao-Xiang*. It concerns the rescue of Kingfisher Phoenix (not Jewel Lotus) from her upturned boat and her reunion with her father at a riverside travel-halt.

20. Zhou Bo was a famous general at the beginning of the Han dynasty. A Yuan *zaju* by Guan Hanqing was called *Empress Dowager Bao races her horse to save Zhou Bo*.

21. There were two Sông *guanben zaju* about Cui Hu, a *zhugongdiao* ballad called *Cui Hu asks for liquid refreshment*, and Yuan *zaju* of the same title by Bai Pu (1226–post 1306) and Shang Zhongxian. Cui Hu, asking one day for a drink of water, met the beautiful Xie Chrysanthemum Beauty whom, after many

vicissitudes, including her death and revival, he married.

22. There is a *zaju* of this title by Shi Junbao (thirteenth century). Qiu Hu fails, after a number of years of absence, to recognize his own wife, and tries to seduce her. The story is a very old one, used, incidentally, as the topic of a show by automata or fantoccini before the Emperor Yangdi (r.605–17). I have translated the Yuan *zaju* and it is the next play in this collection.

23. There is a Yuan *zaju* called *Great Prince Wang's single-sword meeting* by Guan Hanqing. The story is of the famous general Guan Yu and his brave encounter, armed only with a sword, with his wily enemy Lu Su in the midst of the latter's camp.

24. The story tells how Emperor Minghuang (in later ages regarded for other reasons as a patron deity of the theatre!) was forced to leave his capital because of a rebellion and was obliged by his mutinous guard to allow them to trample his beloved Lady Yang, whom they regarded as responsible for the rebellion, under their horses' hooves. The theme was used in a *yuanben* called *Striking the paulownia*; a *zhugongdiao* ballad by playwright Wang Bocheng (thirteenth century); and various Yuan *zaju*, by Guan Hanqing, Bai Pu, Yu Tianxi (thirteenth century) and Yue Bochuan (thirteenth century).

25. There was a *nanxi, Father and son dream at Mancheng travel-halt*, by Wang Yuanheng (fourteenth century), another – possibly the same play – called *Autumn night at Mancheng travel-halt*, and a Yuan *zaju* by Zheng Tingyu (thirteenth century) called *Son and father dream on an autumn night at Mancheng travel-halt*. From surviving *nanxi* songs, it seems they must have been based on a love-story concerning the poet Liu Shiqing.

26. On the theme of the love affair between scholar Zhang Junrui (Zhang Gong) and Cui Little Oriole in the west wing of a Buddhist monastery, around which topic there were a *guzici* ('drum lyric') ballad by Zhao Lingzhi (1051–1107), a Sòng *guanben zaju*, a *yuanben*, a *zhugongdiao* ballad (written around 1200) by Dong Jie-yuan (late twelfth to early thirteenth century), and the Yuan *zaju West wing* by Wang Shifu (thirteenth to early fourteenth century), the latter being the most famous of all Chinese plays.

27. The story of how a woman saved her husband from bad company and bad habits by killing a dog and passing it off as a human corpse. There is an anonymous Yuan *zaju* with this title and on this theme, and there were also *nanxi*, including one attributed to Xiao Dexiang (fourteenth century), and a *chuanqi*(?) attributed to Xu Ji (fourteenth century).

28. There was a Yuan *zaju* called *Four times not knowing on a moonlit night Maid Jing casts blame* by Peng Bocheng (thirteenth century) or Guo Andao (thirteenth century), and possibly another anonymous Yuan *zaju*, as well as a *nanxi* called *Maid Jing blames the swallow for sending the letter.* The story probably concerned the friendship of the founder emperor of the Sòng dynasty with Maid Jing, and how she died for love of him.

29. A *nanxi* play called *Top Graduate Zhang Xie* still survives. It tells how Zhang Xie is helped by Poor Maiden to recover from wounds received at the hands of a brigand, and marries her, but later, when he becomes Top Graduate, deserts her for a minister's daughter. When he meets Poor Maiden again he even tries to kill her with his sword. In the end he is, however, obliged to marry Poor Maiden once more!

30. Probably on the tale of how Princess Lechang and her lover each took part of a broken mirror as a token when they were separated, and after many vicissitudes were reunited through the rejoining of the two parts of the mirror. There were one or more *nanxi* on the topic, called *Lechang breaks the mirror*, one existing before 1324 and probably before 1276. There was also a Yuan *zaju* called *Story of Lechang's dividing of the mirror* by Shen He (d. 1330).

31. There were a *guanben zaju*; a *yuanben*; a *zhugongdiao* ballad; and a Yuan *zaju* by Bai Pu and a *nanxi* both called by the above title. All were on the same theme, that of the young scholar out riding on horseback who catches sight over a wall of a beautiful young lady, with whom, after a troubled marriage, he eventually finds happiness. In the Yuan *zaju* the young lady is holding a sprig of 'green-plum' blossom, but it is mentioned that she throws fruit.

32. There were a Yuan *zaju* by Wang Zhongwen (early thirteenth century), and a *nanxi* both with this title. The story seems to have been of a talented scholar's meeting a beautiful young lady in the pavilion and writing a poem there to express some regrets, and of their eventual happy marriage.

33. There were a *guanben zaju* and a *yuanben* on this theme. The story was that of a wicked Buddhist monk who became enamoured of a married woman and deliberately made a mistake in sending her a letter. The husband discovered the letter and divorced his wife, whereupon the monk took his opportunity to try to marry her. But he was unmasked and punished. Perhaps the handkerchief was the woman's love-token to the monk?

34. There were Yuan *zaju* by Guan Hanqing and by Wang Shifu,

the latter still extant, as well as *nanxi* – one southern play by an anonymous playwright of the early Ming still survives – all having the above title. A Yuan *zaju* by Ma Zhiyuan (thirteenth, possibly to early fourteenth century) may have dealt with the same events, and a *yuanben* certainly did. The story tells how the poor scholar Lü Mengzheng married a wealthy young beauty, but both of them were cast out by her father and forced to go and live in a broken-down kiln, from whence he had to brave fierce snowstorms to go and beg charity food from a temple. I translate a play embodying some events of this story later in this collection.

35. From surviving songs of a *nanxi* play called *Yang Shi and the brocade perfume sachet*. The story would seem to have been of a love-affair between Yang Shi and the singing-girl Han Jewel Child.

36. There is a Yuan *zaju* by Ji Junxiang (thirteenth century) and a Yuan or early Ming anonymous *nanxi* or *chuanqi* with this title. The *zaju*, in translation, was one that had a great influence on eighteenth-century European literature and on Voltaire in particular.

37. The theme is that of Liu Bei, ruler of the Kingdom of Wei, escaping from deadly peril by leaping his horse across the wide Sandalwood Stream. The theme was used for another item in the fantoccini or automata show of Emperor Yangdi (see note 19 above), and also in a Yuan *zaju* by Gao Wenxiu (thirteenth century) and a *yuanben*, both called *Meeting at Xiangyang*.

38. The story of how thunder, or a thunder-god, destroyed a stone tablet bearing an inscription from the handwriting of a famous ancient calligrapher. There is a Yuan *zaju* sometimes attributed to Ma Zhiyuan called *At midnight thunder roars and destroys the Recommending Blessings stone tablet*.

39. The 'kills' is perhaps a mistake for 'teaches'. There was a Yuan *zaju* called *Bing Ji teaches his son and sets up Xuandi* by Guan Hanqing, and another one possibly on the same subject by Li Kuanfu (thirteenth century). Bing Ji (d.55 BC) was historically an official at the Han court who managed to rescue the infant who became the Emperor Xuandi (73–58 BC). The incident of the teaching or killing is not known.

40. This must have concerned that famous ancient paragon of filial love, Lao Lai-zi, who when seventy used to dress up in motley clothing and play children's games to remind his aged parents of the happy days when he was still their infant and thus bring them joy.

41. The story tells how the famous mandarin and judge Bao Zheng was sent to Chenzhou to right injustice and to distribute grain to the people there. There is a Yuan or early Ming anonymous *zaju* called *Academician Bao sells grain at Chenzhou*. Lu Dengshan (early fourteenth century) wrote a *zaju* called *Opening the granary and selling the grain* which is possibly the same one.

42. The theme was that of the mother of the famous philosopher Mencius, who when he was a child thrice moved house in order that he might grow up under the right moral influences. There was a Yuan *zaju* called *Mother Meng thrice moves* by some unknown playwright.

43. The stage direction adds 'in different guise'. This probably indicates that the same one actor doubles as both valet and Wang Sishen.

44. There is a stage direction seemingly indicating that Dogson sings, but the text seems confused at this point, and there is in fact no stage direction indicating that Golden Notice sings or says the following first verse.

45. Lit. 'fly-head profit' and 'empty snail-horn fame', both phrases earlier used by the celebrated poet Su Dongpo (1036–1101).

46. Lit. 'Doctor Tea', a common term for a tea-house keeper or waiter in a tea-house.

47. i.e. the fabulous islands of Penglai, Fangzhang and Yingzhou, where immortals were said to dwell; i.e., far and wonderful places.

48. This can refer to various things, but here probably to the five major lakes of China, i.e. from all over the land.

49. A famous poet of the early thirteenth century. He was a friend and relative of some famous Yuan *zaju* playwrights and also wrote a famous poem about a peasant farmer visiting a theatre for the first time to watch a *yuanben* and Yuan *zaju*. From the above line, he must have been an actor himself too.

50. Zheng Yuanhe, the hero of a famous love story used in several plays, was once forced to beg for his living.

51. Liu Shuahe was a famous actor of the early thirteenth century, and also the father-in-law of two Yuan *zaju* actor-playwrights. Other sources mention him as a *yuanben* actor, as well as a *zaju* actor.

52. A part-guess. Possibly it means a young boy, or a supporting male role?

53. There is an anonymous Yuan *zaju* of this title (the text of the above play mistakenly reads 'sugar' instead of 'load'. I have

corrected it), and there was an anonymous Yuan *zaju* called *Story of Cinnabar*, which may have been the same play or on the same theme. The story is of the murder of a trader in cinnabar. Before he killed him, his murderer told him that some water-bubbles on the eaves above them were the only things that would seek justice for him, implying that he could not hope for justice, but supernatural forces eventually punished the killer.

54. There was a *zaju* of this title by Guan Hanqing. See note 23.

55. There was a *zaju* of this name by Guan Hanqing. The story is of Guan Ning, a scholarly paragon who, shocked at his friend's lack of zeal for study, cut in two the sitting-mat which they had hitherto shared.

56. Why 'variant', I am not sure. Possibly there was an earlier play and this one shifted the emphasis of the plot? There was a Yuan *zaju* by Hua Li-lang (thirteenth century), actor-playwright son-in-law of Liu Shuahe, called *Chancellor's court*, and one, possibly the same, called *Rough-tough Zhang Fei plays havoc in the chancellor's court*. The story must have been that of the coarse warrior-hero Zhang Fei and his riotous behaviour in the residence of Cao Cao, the Han chancellor.

57. Most probably the 'evading' should be 'snatching'. There is a Yuan *zaju* called *Thrice snatching the lance* by Shang Zhongxian (thirteenth century). In it the warrior hero Yuchi Jingde in three bouts during a tournament against a prince, his deadly enemy, thrice nimbly snatches the lance from the prince's hands, thus shaming him.

58. There was an anonymous Yuan *zaju* called *Academician Bao in the snowstorm*.

59. There was an anonymous Yuan *zaju* called *Liu Chen mistakenly deserts his wife*.

60. There is a Yuan *zaju* of this title by Zheng Guangzu (late thirteenth to early fourteenth century) and another was less reliably attributed to Guan Hanqing. The story is of the prime minister Yi Yin's loyal service to King Tang of the Shang dynasty.

61. There was an anonymous Yuan *zaju* of this title. In a number of cases, however – including this one – the Yuan *zaju* I have mentioned in the notes above are first recorded in an early Ming work which may conceivably have culled the titles from the present *nanxi*!

62. A regular characteristic of the clown or butt's performance in *yuanben*, as witnessed by, among other things, a surviving Sông tile picture and a Yuan clay model of an actor.

63. Probably comic noises that were part of the *yuanben* clown's stock-in-trade?

64. Perhaps connected in theme with the *nanxi* and *zaju* on Maid Jing, see note 28.

65. There were many variants of this *yuanben*, of which I translate one at the beginning of this collection. They were often inserted in Yuan and Ming *zaju* and *nanxi* as a comic interlude sometimes barely connected with the main plot.

66. Some texts give 'woman' or 'wife' instead of 'rake'.

67. There was a *guanben zaju* called *Two get on well together and ten thousand years' fragrance*. Sometimes this title is regarded as joined on to the previous one.

68. Huang Luzhi was another name of the famous poet and statesman Huang Tingjian (1045–1105), but I have not identified the story.

69. Bright King Ma was a god or demon, and may have been the same deity as Horse-headed Maid (Ma-tou-niang), goddess of silkworms. The latter, while still a mortal, was by her mother promised in marriage to a horse. Her father slew the horse and flayed it. The horse-hide wrapped itself round the girl and flew off with her. She then changed into a silkworm and became deified. Possibly the play concerned this story, for there was a *guanben zaju* called *Horse-head. Bright King Ma* is also found as a *yuanben* title in another Yuan work.

70. This *yuanben* is also mentioned in another Yuan work. Its story must have been that of Zhu Mian (d.1126), who hunted for huge ornamental rocks with which to win the emperor's favours and was partly responsible for a subsequent rebellion.

71. Meaning doubtful. 'Compose' or 'write comedy'?

72. 'Write' can also mean 'copy' in the Chinese here. In taking plays from other troupes, speed might be essential, but so it might for other forms of competition.

73. i.e. Dadu, present-day Peking. This is the most solid indication that such societies, sometimes at least, furnished the Yuan troupes with their acting material.

74. There was a Yuan *zaju* by Gao Wenxiu called *Chaining Water Mother*, and Xu Zishou (late fourteenth century) is said to have written one called *Drowning Water Mother*. The story concerned the taming of an irate water deity of Sizhou (in Anhwei province) by a Buddhist immortal called Novice Mucha. 'Prop-stunts' is an attempt at translating *qi*, a kind of performance sometimes involving the rapid exchange of quips, but sometimes, perhaps, also having something to do with the other meaning of *qi*: 'stage-props'. Possibly in the

latter sense the performance mentioned here could have involved the dexterous handling of props (chains? weapons?). Another Yuan work mentions a *Water Mother qi yuanben*.

75. Another Yuan work mentions *Youthful wanderings* (also found as a *ci* tune-title) as a *shuanchu yanduan*, a category of *yuanben*, seemingly a briefer than usual kind of *yuanben*. The *shuan* is used also in the text above, and I translate it as 'sketch'.

76. Perhaps this refers to acrobatic fighting, and perhaps rather to *Water Mother* than to *Youthful wanderings*, if it is not just a general reference to such fighting acrobatics in *yuanben* performances.

77. *Zhanggu*, a narrow-waisted wood-framed drum, decorated with colourful embroidered ribbons and played with the left hand and a stick in the right.

78. These would be the actors playing Dogson and Sishen (and valet), plus a *chou*-clown, but the first two must be playing a different part here. 'Suspend the stage' perhaps means some kind of slapstick or farcical interlude.

Qiu Hu tries to seduce his own wife

1. There is debate as to the precise purpose of 'end-titles' and 'preliminary titles' (see page 30). Advertising may have been part of their function. Each half of the end-titles had a separate designation, the first being called a 'theme item' and the second a 'main title'.

'Secret liaison with Chancellor Bo Pi'

1. The 'vermilion bird' was an ancient symbol for the south of China.

2. Perhaps he says '*south* of the city walls' simply because of a famous Han poem concerning do-or-die fighting and the aftermath of battle, which was called 'Fighting south of the city walls'.

3. An anatomical term used in acupuncture, the points at which acupuncture is best applied.

Wolf of Mount Zhong

1. A philosopher who lived about 479–381 BC. He taught a way of

life which urged 'universal love' to all without partially, and which was opposed to aggressive violence. In his principles he clashed to some extent with the Confucian school of philosophy, and this play subjects Mo-ist attitudes to satire as being foolishly impractical and self-destructive.

2. Both these terms derive from the Confucian philosopher Mencius, or were used by him. Treacherous ministers and rebellious sons were most heinous villains in Confucian eyes.
3. Lit. 'raven's head', a term for aconite, monk's-hood, or wolf's-bane, i.e. 'poisonous'!
4. Which advocated a love towards others that was determined by the nature of one's relationship to them.
5. The Chinese phrase comes from the *Analects* of Confucius, and must have a certain ironic or comic effect here.

Hegemon King says farewell to his queen

1. In Shantung province.
2. Sun Wu and Wu Qi, both Zhou dynasty military leaders and famous as the authors of two of the most noted Chinese treatises on the arts of warfare.
3. In present Shensi province.
4. The dynastic house that ruled the Qin had the name Ying.
5. The Six States being the Zhou states of Qi, Chu, Yan, Zhao, Han and Wei.
6. A tributary of the River Bian in Honan province, now known as River Jialu, and originally dug on the orders of the First Emperor of Qin. Xiang Yu and Liu Bang of Han divided the world between them along this frontier.
7. Chen Yu (died 204 BC) was a Confucian. He and his great friend Zhang Er were wanted men under the Qin. Chen later rose to the position of Regent under the King of Zhao, while Zhang Er surrendered to the Han and joined Han Xin in the conquering of Zhao and killing of Chen Yu.
8. In present Hopeh province.
9. Regions in present Anhwei province.
10. Liu Bang; the House of Liu being associated with the element of fire in certain cosmological theories of the five elements.
11. i.e. Gaixia, a place in present Anhwei province where Xiang Yu met his death.
12. As note 11.
13. It was an ancient custom to remove the left ear of an enemy.
14. Zhang Liang (died 189 BC) was a famous strategic adviser of Liu Bang's.

15. Key military place in present Honan province, under Han control.
16. Another key military place in Honan, under Han control.
17. A city in present Kiangsu province. It was where Xiang Yu set himself up as Hegemon King of Western Chu, and where he made his capital.
18. This refers to the famous story of the foolish farmer who, seeing a rabbit break its neck by bumping into a tree-stump, downed tools and sat by the stump fully expecting a rich harvest of rabbits for his dinners. Here the reference simply means 'a foolish, passive, wait-and-see approach'.
19. A term for the moon, or moonlight. Legend held that a toad lived in the moon. The terms 'Toad' and 'Toad Palace' were also used for the moon. Presumably the term arose because of the markings observable on the face of the moon, as in the case of the Man in the Moon.
20. The last king of the Shang dynasty, who reigned until 1027 BC.
21. The king who overthrew King Zhou and founded the Zhou dynasty. He reigned 1027–1025 BC.
22. Liu Bang's home region, in present Kiangsu province.
23. In Honan province. In 203 BC, Chu forces inflicted a heavy defeat on Han there.